AMERICA'S BEST
HARVEST PIES

AMERICA'S BEST
HARVEST PIES

THE AMERICAN PIE COUNCIL WITH LINDA HOSKINS

APPLE, PUMPKIN, BERRY, AND MORE!

Skyhorse Publishing

Skyhorse Publishing books may be purchased in bulk at special discounts for sales promotion, corporate gifts, fund-raising, or educational purposes. Special editions can also be created to specifications. For details, contact the Special Sales Department, Skyhorse Publishing, 307 West 36th Street, 11th Floor, New York, NY 10018 or info@skyhorsepublishing.com.

Skyhorse® and Skyhorse Publishing® are registered trademarks of Skyhorse Publishing, Inc.®, a Delaware corporation.

Visit our website at www.skyhorsepublishing.com.

10 9 8 7 6 5 4 3 2 1

Library of Congress Cataloging-in-Publication Data is available on file.

ISBN: 978-1-62636-259-8

Printed in China

Introduction

When I tell people I'm the executive director of the American Pie Council, they think I'm kidding. "What a great job," they say. And it *is* a great job! The people I meet—from those who work at commercial pie manufacturing facilities to restaurant chefs to home bakers—are terrific, and we all have one thing in common: *We love pie!*

The American Pie Council, founded in 1983, is the only organization dedicated solely to pie, America's favorite dessert. We believe in the total enjoyment, consumption, and pursuit of pie. We believe that the art of pie making shouldn't be forgotten. We believe that the enjoyment of pie should be continued. We believe that the pursuit of finding the perfect pie should be eternal. And it is in this spirit that we hold the American Pie Council Crisco National Pie Championships every year to determine who makes the best pies in America.

In the months before the event, two hundred judges (food professionals, chefs, cookbook authors, food editors, suppliers to the pie industry, and everyday pie lovers) are chosen, and in April each year, pie bakers from all over the country descend upon Celebration, Florida to compete. Pies are entered into five divisions: commercial, independent/retail bakers, amateur bakers, professional chefs, and junior chefs, and then further divided into price point and flavor categories. Then, the judging begins. Close to 1,000 pies are judged each year over the course of three days, each entrant hoping his or her pie will be the best!

As the Executive Director of the American Pie Council, I have the opportunity to taste many different kinds of pies, but my favorites are always the ones made with fresh fruit. To get the best tasting pie it is important to use fresh fruits that are in season.

Paying attention to the fruits that are in season in your part of the country becomes an important part of making a great pie. America's Best Harvest Pies brings you almost 80 award winning recipes from the National Pie Championships that use fresh fruits. I hope to meet you some day at the National Pie Championships.

❧ CONTENTS ❧

Apple

Gratz Grand Apple Pecan Caramel Pie

Heidi CV Neidlinger, Schuylkill Haven, PA 2006 APC Crisco National Pie Championships Amateur Division 3rd Place

Ingredients

CRUST

2 cups plus 4 tablespoons all-purpose flour

2 tablespoons sugar

1 teaspoon salt

8 tablespoons (4 oz.) cream cheese, chilled and cut into ½ inch cubes

8 tablespoons frozen butter

4 tablespoons frozen Crisco

6 to 10 tablespoons ice-cold water

GLAZE

¼ cup packed brown sugar

1 tablespoon butter, melted

1 tablespoon light corn syrup

1 cup whole pecan halves

FILLING

4 to 5 pounds Granny Smith apples, peeled, cored, and sliced

¼ cup sugar and a sprinkle of cinnamon

½ cup packed brown sugar

3 tablespoons flour

¾ teaspoon cinnamon

Dash ground nutmeg

Directions

For the crust: Mix flour, sugar, and salt in a medium bowl. Rub the cream cheese into the flour mixture until it resembles cornmeal. Grate the butter and shortening into the mixture. Mix again until it resembles cornmeal. Stir in the ice-cold water a little at a time with a fork until the dough clumps and you can form a ball. Make two balls, cover with plastic wrap, and refrigerate overnight.

For the glaze: Combine brown sugar, butter, and corn syrup. Spread this mixture evenly into greased glass pie plate. Arrange whole pecan halves in a circle pattern by size around the entire dish, completely covering the glaze. Set aside.

Remove dough ball from refrigerator and shape into a disc. Roll out on a floured board into a 14-inch circle and then place into the glass dish on top of the prepared glaze and nuts, fitting sides and bottom of dish. Let edges hang over until filling is ready. Refrigerate until ready to use.

For the filling: Preheat oven to 425°F. Mix sliced apples with sugar and sprinkle with cinnamon. In a large skillet, cook apples about 10 minutes until slightly tender and set aside. In a small mixing bowl, mix brown sugar, flour, cinnamon, and nutmeg, then set aside. Remove prepared crust with glaze from refrigerator. Take half of the cooked apples and spread evenly into the crust that is sitting on top of the nuts/glaze. Then sprinkle evenly with ½ of the flour/sugar mixture. Repeat this process with remaining apples and flour mixture.

Take second dough ball out of refrigerator and roll out onto floured surface into a 14-inch circle. Place on top of apples. Take sides of both crusts and tuck under. Flute edges of pie. With a knife, cut slits into top of pie to vent. Cover edges with pie ring and bake 50 to 60 minutes. Put pie on cooling rack when done baking. After only 5 minutes, flip pie onto a heat-proof plate, and let cool totally before serving (about 2 hours).

Simply Divine Cinnamon Roll Raisin Apple Pie

Karen Hall, Elm Creek, NE 2011 APC Crisco National Pie Championships Amateur Division 1st Place Apple

Ingredients

CRUST

3 cups unbleached flour

1 cup plus 1 tablespoon butter-flavored Crisco, cold

½ teaspoon baking powder

1 egg

1 teaspoon sea salt

¼ cup plus 1 tablespoon ice water

1 tablespoon sugar

1 tablespoon rice vinegar

FILLING

7 apples, peeled, cored, and thinly sliced

⅓ cup butter, melted

¾ cup granulated sugar

½ cup light brown sugar, packed

1½ teaspoons cinnamon

2 tablespoons flour

½ cup raisins

CINNAMON ROLL TOP

8 oz. package refrigerated crescent rolls

2 tablespoons butter, melted

2 tablespoons sugar

2 teaspoons cinnamon

ICING FOR CINNAMON ROLL TOP

2 oz. cream cheese, softened

1 cup powdered sugar

1 tablespoon butter, softened

1 tablespoon milk

Directions

For the crust: In a large bowl, combine flour, baking powder, salt, and sugar. With a pastry blender, cut in Crisco until mixture resembles coarse crumbs. In a small bowl, beat egg, water, and vinegar together. Add egg mixture slowly to flour mixture while tossing with fork until mixture is moistened. Do not overmix. Divide dough and shape into 3 balls, flattening each to form 3 discs. Wrap each disc with plastic wrap and refrigerate at least 30 minutes before using. Makes 3 single crusts. Use one disc for this recipe.

For the filling: Preheat oven to 425°F. In a large skillet over low heat, melt butter. In a large bowl, blend together granulated sugar, brown sugar, cinnamon, and flour. Add apples and raisins to mixture and toss to coat apples. Turn apple mixture into skillet with melted butter; cook and stir over medium heat for 6 to 8 minutes or until apples are tender.

Roll out bottom crust and line 9-inch pie dish; flute edge.

Turn filling into pastry-lined dish; protect edge of pie with foil and bake at 425°F for 10 minutes. Reduce oven to 375°F and bake an additional 10 minutes.

For the topping: Unroll crescent rolls (do not divide); brush top side with 2 tablespoons melted butter. Blend together sugar and cinnamon in a small bowl; sprinkle mixture over melted butter. Roll crescent pastry up into a log lengthwise and pinch edge to seal. Cut log into ¼ inch miniature cinnamon rolls. Place miniature cinnamon rolls evenly on top of pie. Bake at 375°F degrees 18–20 minutes longer or until cinnamon roll top is golden brown. Cool pie on rack.

For the icing: In a small bowl, blend together until smooth the softened cream cheese, powdered sugar, butter, and milk. Pipe icing onto cinnamon rolls in a swirling pattern.

Harvest Apple Pie

Lana Ross, Indianola, IA 2009 APC Crisco National Pie Championships Amateur Division 1ˢᵗ Place Apple

Ingredients

CRUST

2 cups flour

1 teaspoon salt

²/₃ cups Crisco

6–8 tablespoons ice-cold water

2 teaspoons vinegar

FILLING

3 Harrelson apples, peeled, cored, and sliced

3 Golden Delicious apples, peeled, cored, and sliced

¹/₃ cup flour

1 cup sugar

2 teaspoons cinnamon

½ cup dried cranberries

TOPPING

1 cup flour

6 tablespoons butter

½ cup brown sugar

²/₃ cups toasted, sliced almonds

Ice water

Directions

For the crust: Mix together flour and salt. Mix the vinegar into the ice water. Cut the Crisco into the flour mixture and gradually add water until dough sticks together. Roll out half and place in a nine- or ten-inch pie pan. Trim and flute the edges. Roll out the remaining dough and make decorative leaf cutouts for top crust.

For the filling: Preheat the oven to 350°F. In a bowl, combine the flour, sugar, cinnamon, and cranberries. Add the apples. Toss to coat and place into prepared crust.

For the topping: Combine all topping ingredients and carefully cover the apples. Add the cut-out leaves around the crust. Dampen the crust edge with the ice water to help leaves stick. Bake at 350°F for 75 to 80 minutes.

Apple Pie

Michael Glodowski, Verona, WI 2011 APC Crisco National Pie Championships Amateur Division 3rd place Apple

Ingredients

CRUST

2 cups flour

1 teaspoon salt

¾ cup butter

5 to 6 tablespoons water

FILLING

1 tablespoon lemon juice

6 cups apples (2 each Granny Smith, Braeburn, McIntosh, and Fuji), peeled, cored, and cut into small pieces

1½ cups sugar

2 tablespoons minute tapioca

1 teaspoon salt

1 teaspoon cinnamon

2 tablespoons flour

1 tablespoon cornstarch

3 tablespoons butter

1 egg

1 tablespoon sugar

Directions

To make the crust: Combine flour, salt, and butter by crossing 2 knives or using a pastry blender until the consistency of the mixture resembles pea-sized balls. Add water to blend. Roll out on a floured surface to form two 9-inch crusts. Place one crust in a 9-inch pie dish. Set the other aside for the top crust.

To make the filling: Preheat oven to 450°F. Combine lemon juice and apples to coat. Add sugar, tapioca, salt, cinnamon, flour, and cornstarch and combine. Pour filling into prepared bottom crust, top with butter and cover with prepared top crust. Score top crust to vent. Mix egg with pastry brush and spread over top crust to lightly coat. Sprinkle sugar over egg coating. Bake at 450°F for 15 minutes. Reduce heat to 350°F. Continue baking until filling bubbles in center of pie, approximately 45 to 60 minutes.

Best Ever Caramel Apple Pecan Pie

Rumie Martinez, Farwell, MI 2010 APC Crisco National Pie Championships Amateur Division 3rd Place Apple

Ingredients

CRUST

1 cup flour

½ cup Crisco shortening

½ teaspoon salt

¼ cup cold milk (approximately)

FILLING

½ cup Kraft caramel bits from an 11
    oz. bag. Save the rest for garnish
    below.
    [Note: Kraft caramel bits work
    best, otherwise, unwrap and cut up
    12 regular Kraft caramels each into
    8 tiny pieces]

3 lbs, minimum 8 cups, of apples
    (Golden Delicious or Jonagold),
    peeled, cored, and sliced

⅔ cup firmly packed brown sugar

1 tablespoon fresh lemon juice

2 tablespoons granulated sugar

2 tablespoons cornstarch

1 teaspoon ground cinnamon

1 teaspoon pure vanilla extract

¼ teaspoon ground nutmeg

PECAN CRUMB TOPPING

¾ cup all-purpose flour

½ cup chopped pecan halves

½ cup granulated sugar

¼ teaspoon salt

8 tablespoons unsalted butter,
    slightly cold

CARAMEL GARNISH

Remaining Kraft caramels

4 tablespoons unsalted butter

1½ tablespoons water

¼ to ½ cup chopped pecans

12 pecan halves

Directions

For the crust: Cut shortening into the flour and salt until it resembles coarse crumbs about the size of a pea. Add in cold milk a little at a time. When it starts to ball up and you have no dry ingredients visible, then your crust is ready to roll out on a floured non-stick silicone mat (or floured surface). Put your bottom crust into a 9-inch pie dish, then trim and flute the edges of your crust. Layer ½ cup of caramel bits on the bottom crust in the pie dish and set this aside in your refrigerator to cool.

For the filling: Preheat oven to 400°F. Mix together apples, brown sugar, and lemon juice in a large bowl. Set aside for about 5 minutes to juice. Mix the granulated sugar and cornstarch together in a small bowl. Once mixed, combine with the apples and mix together. Add the cinnamon, nutmeg, and vanilla to the apples and mix well. Fill the chilled crust with apple mixture, mounding the apples in pie dish as high as you can. Pat down the fruit and smooth down the apples so none are sticking up. Place the pie on the center rack and bake for 30 minutes.

For the topping: While pie is baking, make the crumb topping by combining flour, chopped pecans, granulated sugar, and salt. Cut in butter. Once mixture is coarse, knead together with hands so butter is well blended and looks gravelly. Keep in refrigerator until the pie comes out of the oven.

After 30 minutes of baking, remove pie from oven, lower temperature to 350°F. Carefully pile the refrigerated pecan topping on top and in the center of pie. Spread crumb topping over entire pie evenly to edge of crust. Tap down the crumb topping, and then return the pie to the oven for an additional 45 to 50 minutes. Juices will bubble thickly around the edge of pie toward the end of baking time. Place a baking sheet or tin foil sheet under the pie in oven to catch any juices. You can use a pie shield or tin foil if your pie is getting too dark. Remove pie from oven and cool for approximately 45 to 60 minutes on a wire rack.

For the garnish: While pie is cooling, prepare the caramel garnish. Using a double boiler, combine the butter, water, and remaining caramels. Slowly melt the caramels over simmering water. This should take about 10 to 15 minutes. As caramels are slowly melting, carefully press down and mix together with the melting butter and water. When melted and smooth, mix together and drizzle the caramel garnish mixture over the pie after it has cooled. Immediately sprinkle the chopped pecans over the top and place the pecan halves decoratively on top of pie. Let the pie finish cooling for at least 3 to 4 hours.

Apple Leaf Pie

Sarah Spaugh, Winston-Salem, NC 2004 APC Crisco National Pie Championships Amateur Division 2ⁿᵈ Place Apple

Ingredients

CRUST

3 cups all-purpose flour

1 teaspoon salt

¾ cup butter-flavored Crisco

¼ cup cold butter, cut into pieces

6 tablespoons cold water

1 tablespoon white vinegar

1 egg, beaten

FILLING

7 cups apples, peeled, cored, and
   sliced

¾ cup white sugar

¼ cup brown sugar

¾ cup apple juice

1 teaspoon cinnamon

¼ teaspoon allspice

2 tablespoons butter

2 tablespoons cornstarch

1 tablespoon maple syrup

Half and half to brush over crust

Directions

For the crust: Combine flour and salt in a mixing bowl. Cut in shortening and butter until coarse crumbs form. Combine water and beaten egg; add vinegar. Stir egg mixture into flour mixture with a fork. Divide dough into 2 balls. Roll one out for bottom crust. Roll out the other and make leaf cutouts for top of pie.

For the filling: Preheat oven to 400°F. Combine apples, spices, and sugars in a mixing bowl. Combine cornstarch and apple juice in a small saucepan. Bring to a slight boil. Add butter and maple syrup. Pour over apples and mix. Slowly heat mixture in a large saucepan until apples are barely tender. Spoon filling into unbaked pie shell. Moisten edges of crust with water. To assemble top crust over filling, start from the outside edge and cover the apples with a ring of leaves. Place a second ring of leaves above, staggering positions. Continue with rows of leaves until filling is covered. Place tiny balls of dough in center. Brush lightly with half and half. Bake at 400°F for 10 minutes, then 350°F for 30 to 40 minutes or until crust is golden brown.

Splendid Apple Pie

Therese "Josie" Chaffee, Longmont, CO 2010 APC Crisco National Pie Championships Amateur Division 1ˢᵗ Place Apple

Ingredients

CRUST

2²/₃ cups all-purpose flour

1½ teaspoons salt

1 cup (one stick) Crisco shortening

½ cup plus 1 tablespoon ice water

FILLING

7 medium Braeburn or sweet/tart
  apples, peeled, cored, and thinly
  sliced

1 tablespoon fresh lemon juice

²/₃ cup Splenda sugar blend

2 teaspoons ground cinnamon

3 tablespoons all-purpose flour

¼ teaspoon salt

CRUMB TOPPING

½ cup Splenda brown sugar blend

½ cup all-purpose flour

½ cup Quaker oats

¼ teaspoon salt

½ cup unsalted butter

CARAMEL PECAN FINISH

¼ cup Smucker's sugar-free caramel
  topping

¼ cup chopped pecans

Directions

Makes dough for two pie crusts. Use half for this recipe and save the rest for another pie.

For the crust: Working in a cool place and using cool utensils, sift together flour and salt. With a pastry blender or two knives, cut in half the shortening, until the size of peas, and then cut in the other half until small crumbs are achieved. Gradually drizzle most of the ice water over crumb mixture, while stirring and lifting with a fork to incorporate, until mixture begins to come together.

Gently form a ball and cut pastry in half with knife. Lightly flatten one half into a circular shape. Keeping work surface and rolling pin liberally dusted with flour, gently roll the dough from center out to an 11- to 12-inch circle, occasionally picking up the pastry and dusting the surface and rolling pin with additional flour. If freezing pastry, place unwrapped, formed pastry shell in freezer for 20 minutes before wrapping with foil or plastic. Otherwise, carefully fold pastry in half, place in 9-inch glass pie pan; unfold pastry and ease down into the pie pan; trim any excess, leaving about a ½ inch overhang; fold under edge of pastry; crimp edge.

For the filling: Preheat oven to 450°F. Drizzle lemon juice over sliced apples. Combine Splenda sugar blend, cinnamon, flour, and salt. Toss apples into this mixture. Arrange apple mixture in 9-inch unbaked pie shell.

For the crumb topping: Combine Splenda brown sugar blend, flour, oats, and salt. Cut in butter with pastry blender until they resemble a medium crumb. Carefully spoon mixture on top of apples and gently press onto pie.

Protect bottom of oven with a piece of foil or a pan just large enough to catch drips. Bake at 450°F for 15 minutes; reduce heat to 375°F, cover edge of pie crust with a pie protector or aluminum foil, and continue to bake for an additional 60 minutes. If top is browning too quickly, then loosely cover with foil tent during last 30 minutes of baking time. Remove from oven.

For the topping: While pie is still warm, heat the Smucker's topping and drizzle half the topping over the pie. Sprinkle with pecans, then drizzle the remaining warm Smucker's topping over the pie.

Sweet Cider Apple Pie

Phyllis Bartholomew, Columbus, NE 2010 APC Crisco National Pie Championships Professional Division 1ˢᵗ Place Apple

Ingredients

CRUST

2 cups flour

1 cup cake flour

1 cup Crisco

¼ teaspoon salt

¼ teaspoon baking powder

1 egg

1 tablespoon apple cider vinegar

½ cup ice water

FILLING

3 cups sweet apple cider

4 to 5 Granny Smith apples, peeled, cored, and sliced

2 tablespoons tapioca

¼ teaspoon salt

1 teaspoon cinnamon

²/₃ cup sugar

2 tablespoons melted butter

Directions

For the crust: Mix all the dry ingredients together and then cut in the Crisco. Beat together egg, vinegar, and ice water. Add to the flour mixture. Mix only until all the flour is moistened. Form dough into a ball. Divide in half. Roll out one half for the bottom crust. Roll out the remaining half for a top crust.

For the filling: Preheat oven to 400°F. In a saucepan over medium heat, reduce the apple cider down to about ½ cup. Add the peeled and sliced apples and cook until they are about half-way done. Combine the remaining ingredients and add to the apples.

Pour filling into a pastry-lined pie dish. Add top crust, brush with warm milk and sprinkle with sugar. Bake at 375°F to 400°F for about an hour or until crust is a golden brown color.

Sticky Toffee Pudding Apple Pie

Linda Hundt, DeWitt, MI 2011 APC Crisco National Pie Championships Professional Division 1ˢᵗ Place Crisco Innovation and Best of Show

Ingredients

CRUST

1½ cups flour

¼ teaspoon baking powder

½ teaspoon salt

1 teaspoon sugar

¼ cup cold butter cut in small pieces

½ cup of refrigerated Crisco shortening

STICKY TOFFEE PUDDING
  FILLING

½ cup praline pecans

1 stick of butter, softened

½ cup brown sugar

2 tablespoons heavy cream

1 tablespoon lemon juice

1 egg, beaten

½ cup self-rising flour

APPLE FILLING

5 medium-to-large Michigan Cort-
  land, Ida Red apples, peeled, thinly
  sliced, diced

1 cup brown sugar

3 tablespoons flour

4 tablespoons melted butter

2 teaspoons cinnamon

1 teaspoon lemon juice

¼ teaspoon salt

Homemade Caramel

14 oz. can sweetened condensed milk

1 cup light corn syrup

1 cup sugar

½ cup brown sugar

½ stick butter

1 tablespoon real vanilla extract

CRUMB TOPPING

¾ cup flour

1 cup sugar

¼ teaspoon salt

1 stick butter, softened

PRALINE PECAN GARNISH

1 cup chopped pecans

2 tablespoons butter

2 tablespoons brown sugar

Directions

For the crust: Mix all above ingredients in KitchenAid-style mixer, on medium speed, swiftly until crust appears "pea-like." Carefully sprinkle water into crust mix until it starts to become moistened and gathers together. Pat into a disc. Wrap and refrigerate for at least one half hour. Roll out on to floured surface and make and crimp crust.

For sticky toffee pudding layer: Mix ingredients just until blended. Spread on bottom of pie crust.

For apple filling: Cook ingredients in large pan on medium heat until cooked half-way.

For homemade caramel: In heavy 3-quart saucepan, combine all ingredients but vanilla. Cook over medium heat, stirring constantly, covering all parts of bottom of pan with wire whisk to avoid scorching. Stir until mixture comes to a boil. Reduce heat to low and continue stirring until caramel reaches 244°F on a candy thermometer, or firm-ball stage. Pour into glass container. Cool to use.

Stir in ¾ cup homemade caramel into the apple filling mixture until melted. Pour apple mixture onto the sticky toffee pudding in pie shell.

For crumb topping: Mix together all crumb topping ingredients by hand or a pastry blender until fine and crumbly. Sprinkle pie with crumb topping.

Preheat oven to 400°F. Bake pie for one hour or until knife easily slides into center of pie with no resistance. If pie becomes too brown before done, turn down oven to 350°F to finish baking. Cover with foil completely.

For praline pecan garnish: Melt butter in small pan on medium-low heat until melted. Add pecans and sugar and stir ingredients until you start smelling the nuts roasting. Take off heat and cool. Crumble. Top pie with a generous amount of homemade caramel sauce, praline pecans, and powdered sugar (if desired).

Brandy Apple Pie

Beverly Grey, Celebration, FL 2005 APC Crisco National Pie Championships Amateur Division 1ˢᵗ Place Celebration

Ingredients

CRUST

2 to 2¼ cups flour

1 teaspoon salt

²/₃ cup plus 2 tablespoons shortening

5 to 6 tablespoons cold water

FILLING

6 tablespoons butter

6 to 7 Granny Smith apples (3 lbs. for a big pie plate), peeled, cored, and thinly sliced

½ cup brown sugar

1 cup sugar

2 tablespoons flour or 3 tablespoons cornstarch blended with ¼ cup cold water

1 ½ to 2 teaspoons cinnamon

½ teaspoon nutmeg

¼ teaspoon salt

1 tablespoon whiskey

1 to 2 tablespoons lemon juice

Directions

For the crust: Combine flour and salt in bowl. Cut in shortening until blended and consistency resembles peas. Sprinkle water over surface. Stir with a fork until moistened. Shape into a ball with hands and work until soft (not very long). Roll into two circles. Line pie pan with single crust and fill with apple mixture. Top with single pie crust. Flute edges, cut five slits, and bake as stated below.

For the filling: Preheat oven to 375°F. Place ½ the apples in large skillet with ½ the melted butter and sprinkle with ½ the lemon juice and ½ of the sugars. Cook until tender, stirring often, about seven minutes. Transfer to a large pan. Repeat with rest of butter, apples, lemon juice, and sugars. Add seasonings and flour. Transfer to 10-inch pie plate with a bottom crust. Cover filling with top crust and flute the edges. Cut slits in the top. Brush the top with lightly beaten egg yolk, 2 teaspoons of heavy cream or water. Sprinkle cinnamon and sugar over top. Bake on middle rack on a baking sheet for 40 to 50 minutes or until top is golden. Cool on wire rack for 30 minutes.

Butterscotch Pecan Apple Pie

Bev Johnson, Crookston, MN 2009 APC Crisco National Pie Championships Amateur Division 3rd Place Apple

Ingredients

CRUST
1¼ cups flour
½ teaspoon salt
6 tablespoons unsalted butter
2 tablespoons lard
¼ cup plus 1 tablespoon (if needed)
Ice water

FILLING
7 cups Golden Delicious apples,
    peeled, cored, and sliced
½ cup light brown sugar
1 tablespoon fresh lemon juice
2 tablespoons granulated sugar
1 tablespoon cornstarch
½ teaspoon cinnamon

1 teaspoon vanilla extract

CRUMB TOPPING
¾ cup flour
¾ cup pecan halves
½ cup light brown sugar
¼ teaspoon salt
6 tablespoons unsalted butter (cut
    into ¼ inch pieces)

BUTTERSCOTCH TOPPING
½ cup butterscotch ice cream
    topping
⅓ cup pecan halves
½ cup chopped pecans

Directions

For the crust: Pour water into a spray bottle and place in a bowl of crushed ice to chill. Cut butter and lard into small pieces. Place on two different plates and place in freezer. Place flour and salt in food processor and pulse to mix. Add chilled butter and pulse 8 to 10 times. Add lard and pulse 5 to 7 times. Spray a portion of the water onto the mixture and pulse 3 times, wait 30 seconds and spray again. Continue until all the water is used. Form dough into a ball, knead once or twice, and flatten ball into a ¾ inch disc. Place in bowl and refrigerate for ½ hour. Roll out dough between 2 sheets of plastic wrap or waxed paper. Place in a 9-inch deep dish pie plate. Keep in freezer until ready to use.

For the filling: Preheat oven to 400°F. Combine apples, brown sugar, and lemon juice in a large bowl. Mix well and set aside for 10 minutes to juice. Mix the granulated sugar and cornstarch together and stir into apples along with cinnamon and vanilla.

Pour filling into the chilled pie shell and bake for 30 minutes.

For the crumb topping: Combine flour, pecans, brown sugar, and salt in food processor. Pulse several times, chopping nuts coarsely. Scatter butter over mixture and pulse until they resemble fine crumbs. Place in bowl and mix with fingers until crumbly. Refrigerate until ready to use.

Remove pie from oven and reduce oven temperature to 375°F. Place crumbs in center of the pie and then spread evenly over the top of pie. Tamp down lightly. Return pie to oven so that the part facing the front is now in the back. Bake 40 minutes. Cover the pie with tented foil for the last 15 minutes to keep from getting too brown. Place on wire rack to cool for one hour.

For the butterscotch topping: Warm butterscotch topping in microwave for 15 seconds. Drizzle the topping over pie, press pecan halves into the butterscotch, then sprinkle the chopped pecans over top.

Blueberry

Fresh Blueberry Caramel Crumb Pie

Phyllis Szymanek, Toledo, OH 2010 APC Crisco National Pie Championships Amateur Division 2nd Place Fruit/Berry.

Ingredients

CRUST

1 1/3 cups flour

½ cup Crisco

½ teaspoon salt

3 tablespoons cold water

FILLING

5 cups fresh blueberries

1 cup sugar

1 teaspoon vanilla

3 tablespoons cornstarch

1/8 teaspoon nutmeg

1/8 teaspoon salt

1 tablespoon fresh lemon juice

TOPPING

1 cup light brown sugar

1 cup flour

½ cup chopped walnuts

½ cup quick oats

½ cup butter, cold

¼ cup Smucker's caramel ice cream
   topping

Directions

For the crust: Mix flour and salt in mixing bowl. Add Crisco. With pastry cutter, mix ingredients until mixture resembles coarse crumbs. Add water, one tablespoon at a time, until it forms into a ball. Roll out onto floured surface one inch larger than a 9-inch pie pan. Place into pie plate and flute edges.

For the filling: Combine sugar, cornstarch, nutmeg, and salt in mixing bowl. Add blueberries, vanilla, and lemon juice. Toss to coat. Pour into prepared pie crust.

For the topping: Preheat oven to 425°F. Combine brown sugar, flour, and oats. Cut in butter until crumbly. Add walnuts. Sprinkle over blueberries. Cover edges of crust loosely with foil. Bake at 425°F for 10 minutes, then at 375°F for 45 to 55 minutes. Remove foil the last 15 minutes. Cool on wire rack. Drizzle with Smucker's caramel topping before serving.

Classic Blueberry Pie

Rick Johnson, Belleville, IL 2010 APC Crisco National Pie Championships Amateur Division Fruit/Berry

Ingredients

CRUST

3 cups all-purpose flour

1¼ cups butter

½ teaspoon salt

⅓ cup lard

½ cup cream cheese

½ teaspoon almond extract

FILLING

8 cups frozen blueberries

1½ cups sugar

1 teaspoon cinnamon

½ teaspoon salt

7 tablespoons Clearjel

Directions

For the crust: Combine all ingredients in a food processor and pulse until a ball forms. Chill dough overnight. When ready, roll out 2 crusts. Place one in a pie dish, and place the other to the side for a top crust.

For the filling: Preheat oven to 350°F. Combine blueberries and sugar in a saucepan, and cook on low until juice is released. Strain blueberry mixture, reserving the juice. Continue cooking juice until reduced by half, then add back the blueberries. Add the rest of the ingredients. Fill pie and apply top crust. Cut vents for steam. Bake for approximately 50 minutes.

Blueberry–Cranberry Pie with Pecan Streusel Topping

Susan Asato, Aliso Viejo, CA 2011 APC Crisco National Pie Championships Amateur Division 1ˢᵗ Place Fruit/Berry

Ingredients

CRUST

8 tablespoons Earth Balance vegan butter, chilled (1 stick or 4 oz. by weight)

3 tablespoons Earth Balance vegan shortening, chilled (1.5 oz. by weight)

1 ²/₃ cups all-purpose flour (8 oz. by weight)

2 tablespoons organic sugar

¼ teaspoon salt

3 to 6 tablespoons ice-cold water

FILLING

5 cups blueberries (24 oz. by weight)

2½ cups cranberries (12 oz. by weight)

1 tablespoon lime juice (juice from from 1 to 2 limes)

½ cup sugar (4 oz. by weight, non-bone char processed)

1 tablespoon light brown sugar (non-bone char processed)

6 tablespoons tapioca flour (1.5 oz. by weight)

2 tablespoons all-purpose flour

1 teaspoon cinnamon

½ teaspoon salt

TOPPING

6 tablespoons Earth Balance vegan butter, melted (¾ of a stick or 3 oz. by weight)

1 cup pecans, coarsely chopped (4 oz. by weight)

½ cup rolled oats (1.75 oz. by weight)

²/₃ cup light brown sugar (4 oz. by weight, non-bone char processed)

²/₃ cup all-purpose flour (3 oz. by weight)

½ teaspoon cinnamon

GLAZE

½ cup organic powdered sugar (2.5 oz. by weight, non-bone char processed)

2 to 3 tablespoons lime juice (juice from about 1 lime)

Directions

For the crust: Preheat oven to 350°F. Combine flour, sugar, and salt in the bowl of a food processor. Cut the vegan butter stick and shortening into about ½ inch pieces. Pulse in food processor with flour, sugar, and salt about 10 times or until crumbly. Add 3 to 6 tablespoons ice water (amount will vary depending on kitchen temperature and humidity) and pulse about another 5 times or until mixture holds its shape when a small amount is squeezed in fist. Place dough in an airtight container and refrigerate for at least 1 hour. Roll out dough to about ⅛ inch thickness and press into a 9-inch deep-dish pie plate. Dock bottom with a fork, line with parchment paper, and fill with pie weights. Bake for 14 to 16 minutes or until very lightly browned.

For the filling: When crust has cooled, preheat oven to 375°F. Gently mix together all filling ingredients, then fill pie crust.

For the streusel topping: Mix together all ingredients well using a fork, then spoon evenly over the berry filling. Place pie on a cookie sheet and bake for 20 to 25 minutes, or until the topping and crust edges are browned. Loosely cover the entire pie with aluminum foil. Reduce the temperature to 350°F and bake for an additional 50 to 60 minutes or until the filling just begins to bubble around the edges. Allow to cool for at least 30 minutes.

For the glaze: Whisk together powdered sugar and 2 tablespoons lime juice. Gradually add additional lime juice, several drops at a time as needed, until desired consistency is reached. Drizzle onto cooled pie.

Blueberry & Basil Lime Pie

Linda Hundt, DeWitt, MI 2011 APC Crisco National Pie Championships
Professional Division Fruit/Berry Honorable Mention

Ingredients

CRUST

1 ½ cups flour
¼ teaspoon baking powder
½ teaspoon salt
1 teaspoon sugar
¼ cup cold butter, cut in small pieces
½ cup refrigerated Crisco shortening
Ice water

FILLING

5 cups frozen Michigan blueberries
1 cup sugar
¼ rounded cup cornstarch
3 teaspoons lime juice
½ teaspoon lime zest

6 large basil leaves in cheesecloth bag
2 ½ cups fresh Michigan blueberries,
    slightly mashed

CREAM MIXTURE

1 cup half and half
¼ cup sugar
1 egg
1 teaspoon real vanilla

CRUMB TOPPING

1½ cups flour
2 cups sugar
¼ teaspoon salt
1½ sticks butter, softened

Directions

For the crust: Mix all above ingredients except for the water in Kitchenaid style mixer on medium speed swiftly until dough texture appears "pea-like." Carefully sprinkle water in crust mix until it starts to become moistened and gathers together. Pat into a disc, wrap in plastic, and refrigerate for at least one half-hour. Roll out on to floured surface and place in pie pan. Crimp crust. Freeze until ready to use.

For the filling: Preheat oven to 400°F. Combine 5 cups frozen blueberries, sugar, and cornstarch in a saucepan over medium heat. When mixture begins boiling , add basil leaves bag and boil for 2 minutes, stirring constantly. Remove from heat. Add lime juice and lime zest. Pour 2½ cups of fresh blueberries on bottom of frozen pie crust. Top with blueberry filling.

For the cream mixture: Mix all ingredients well and carefully pour cream mixture on top of blueberry filling.

For the crumb topping: Mix together all crumb topping ingredients by hand or with a pastry blender until fine and crumbly. Top pie with crumb topping, spreading generously around edges.

Bake at 400 °F until filling bubbles over, about 45 minutes to one hour.

The Engagement Ring

Bryan Ehrenholm, Modesto, CA 2011 APC Crisco National Pie Championships Professional Division 1st Place Royal Wedding and Best of Show

Ingredients

The engagement ring worn by Kate Middleton is rich with history and grace, symbolizing the eternal love of Diana for her son William, and William for his future Queen. So this pie is rich with the history of English walnuts and dates, graced by a meringue crust, topped the deep color of blueberries, and encircled with the lightness of whipped cream and diamond dust.

This pie does not have a traditional crust. The meringue will form the crust.

MERINGUE
4 egg whites
1 cup sugar
1 cup vanilla wafers (crushed with
    rolling pin)
1 teaspoon baking powder
1 cup dried English dates (chopped)
1 cup English walnuts (chopped)

TOPPING
2 pints fresh blueberries
1 cup sugar
1/3 cup cornstarch
½ cup water

GARNISH
Whipped cream
Diamond dust (from Michael's Crafts)
    or large kids' "diamond" rings

Directions

For the meringue: Preheat oven to 300°F. Beat egg whites until fluffy. Gradually beat in sugar, fold in wafers, baking powder, dates and walnuts. Pour into a greased pie pan. Bake for 30 minutes. Cool completely. Center will slightly cave, which is normal.

For the topping: Place 1½ cups of water, 1 cup of sugar, and ⅓ cup of corn starch in a small pan. Bring to a boil until thick syrup forms. Cool to room temperature. Mixture should be like a glaze. Toss mixture with blueberries and heap on top of pie, leaving about ½ inch around the edge.

Instructions for the Sparkle: Sprinkle with Diamond Dust or Sparkle Flakes, available at most cake and candy supply stores.

(I purchase from Edwards Cake and Candy Supply at 209-522-2414. They will ship.)

Large candy diamonds are made from a product called Isomalt, which is an inedible sugar product you heat up and put into silicon molds to create the diamonds. Isomalt and molds are available at local cake and candy supply stores and at www.sugarcraft.com. If you don't want to make the diamonds, Sugarcraft sells the actual diamonds pre-made.

Finish pie with whipped topping around edge and garnish with sprinkles. This pie is like eating divinity with blueberries and whipped cream.

Royal Sapphire Blueberry Pie

Susan Boyle, DeBary, FL 2011 APC Crisco National Pie Championships Professional Division Honorable Mention Royal Wedding

Ingredients

VANILLA WAFER CRUMB CRUST

2½ cups of vanilla wafer crumbs, finely crushed

½ cup of butter-flavored Crisco

CREAM FILLING

8 oz. package cream cheese, softened

1/3 cup confectionary sugar

1 teaspoon pure vanilla extract

1/8 teaspoon salt

1 cup whipped topping

BLUEBERRY FILLING

5 cups fresh blueberries

¾ cup water

¾ cup sugar

1/8 teaspoon salt

1/8 teaspoon cinnamon

3 tablespoons flour

1 tablespoon cornstarch

½ tablespoon lemon juice

WHIPPED TOPPING

1 cup heavy whipping cream

½ cup milk

1 tablespoon sugar

Directions

For the crust: Heat oven to 350°F. Combine ingredients until well-blended. Press into pie plate and bake for 10 minutes. Chill until ready to fill.

For the filling: Beat cream cheese, sugar, salt, and vanilla on medium speed until smooth. Add 1 cup of whipped topping. Continue to whip until very thick and smooth.

To bottom chilled vanilla wafer cookie crust, add a layer of cream filling and put back in refrigerator to set while preparing blueberry filling.

For the blueberry filling: In heavy saucepan on medium heat, mix water, cornstarch, flour, sugar, salt, and cinnamon, and stir until mixture starts to thicken. Add lemon juice and continue to stir, adding blueberries to the hot thick mixture. Remove from heat and allow to cool. When cool, spoon on top of cream cheese layer. Pile high for added appeal.

For the whipped topping: Whip ingredients on medium speed in a cold mixing bowl until stiff. Set aside. Garnish pie with whipped topping and blueberries. Optional: Vanilla wafer cookie crumbs or frosted sugar blueberries can be added to the edges or top for that royal look of diamonds and sapphires. Chill several hours before slicing.

Cherry
and Mixed Fruit

Chocolate Cherry Cordial Pie

Christine Montalvo, Windsor Heights, IA 2011 APC Crisco National Pie Championships Amateur Division 1ˢᵗ Place Crisco Classic Cherry

Ingredients

CRUST

1¼ cups all-purpose flour

½ cup sugar

¼ cup unsweetened cocoa

½ teaspoon salt

½ cup Crisco shortening, frozen and
   cut into pieces

3 to 4 tablespoons ice water

FILLING

5 cups frozen cherries

1 cup sugar

¼ cup cornstarch

¼ teaspoon almond extract

2 cups semi-sweet chocolate morsels

½ cup whipping cream

¼ cup butter, cut into pieces

8 oz. package cream cheese,
   softened

¹/₃ cup powdered sugar

1 large egg

8 maraschino cherries with stems

1 cup whipped cream

2 tablespoons powdered sugar

Directions

For the crust: In food processor, add flour, sugar, cocoa, and salt. Pulse to blend. Add Crisco pieces and pulse until mixture resembles cornmeal. Add water and pulse until dough just comes together. Form dough into a disc, wrap in plastic wrap, and chill about 1 hour. Roll out dough to a 12-inch circle between 2 pieces of parchment paper. Spray bottom and sides of a deep-dish 9-inch pie plate with cooking spray. Ease crust into pie plate. Trim and flute edges. Prick bottom of crust with a fork. Line the crust with a piece of aluminum foil and add pie weights, dried beans, or uncooked rice to gently weigh it down. Bake at 425°F for about 20 minutes. Meanwhile, make filling.

For the filling: Preheat oven to 350°F. Place the cherries in 3-quart pot. In small bowl, mix the sugar and cornstarch until well-blended. Stir this into the cherries until evenly combined. Heat over medium heat, stirring constantly until mixture starts to thicken and boil. Let boil for 1 minute. Remove from heat and stir in the almond extract. Set aside and cool completely. Microwave chocolate morsels and cream in a bowl until chocolate begins to melt. Whisk in butter until smooth. Let cool, whisking occasionally for 5 to 10 minutes or until mixture is a spreadable consistency. Spoon half of chocolate mixture into the baked pie crust. Cover and chill remaining chocolate mixture. Spoon cooled cherry mixture evenly over chocolate mixture in pie crust. Set aside.

Beat together cream cheese, sugar, egg, and almond extract at medium speed with an electric mixer until smooth. Pour evenly over cherry pie filling. Bake for 30 minutes or until center is set. Remove pie from oven and cool on a wire rack. Cover and chill for 8 hours.

Microwave reserved chocolate mixture for 1 minute. Stir until spreadable. Dip maraschino cherries in chocolate mixture and let them firm up on a sheet of wax paper for 15 minutes before decorating pie. Spread remaining chocolate evenly over top of pie. In a large bowl, whip cream and sugar until stiff peaks form. Pipe around edge of pie; place cherries decoratively on top of the pie.

Cherry Streusel Pie

Grace Thatcher, Delta, OH 2011 APC Crisco National Pie Championships Amateur Division 2nd Place Crisco Classic Cherry

Ingredients

CRUST

2 cups flour

½ teaspoon salt

10 tablespoons Crisco shortening

3 to 4 tablespoons cold water

STREUSEL

6 tablespoons sugar

4 tablespoons flour

2 teaspoons wheat germ

2 tablespoons almond flour

1/8 teaspoon cinnamon

5 tablespoons butter, melted

2 drops almond extract

¼ cup slivered almonds

FILLING

(2) 15 oz. cans tart cherries, drained, with juice reserved

1 tablespoon clear jel

1 cup dried tart cherries

2 tablespoons almond pastry filling

1 tablespoon butter

Directions

For the crust: Preheat oven to 425°F. In a large mixing bowl, sift together the flour and salt. Then add all of the shortening. Cut the Crisco shortening into the flour with a pastry blender until the mixture develops a coarse texture. Sprinkle the water over the mixture a spoonful at a time, and toss until the dough begins to come together. Gather the dough into a ball and press together with your hands, cover with plastic wrap, and refrigerate for at least one hour before using. Prepare pie crust in a 9-inch pie pan and prebake for 10 to 15 minutes.

For the streusel: Mix sugar, flour, wheat germ, almond flour, and cinnamon together in a medium bowl. Melt butter in a small bowl and add almond extract. Mix lightly, then incorporate into the dry mixture. Add almonds and lightly toss with fingertips to combine, then set aside.

For the filling: Preheat oven to 350°F. Prepare cherry filling by tossing both kinds of cherries together in a bowl. Put reserved cherry juice into a saucepan and reduce to ½ cup. Then add clear jel and simmer for approximately one minute or until thickened. Add to cherry mixture and stir until well-incorporated and allow to cool. In the meantime, mix almond filling with 1 tablespoon melted butter and spread evenly on the bottom of prepared Crisco classic crust.

Add cherry filling and bake for 30 minutes, then place streusel on top and bake an additional 10 minutes, or until slightly browned.

Black Bottom Cherry Pie

Johnna Poulson, Celebration, FL 2005 APC Crisco National Pie Championships Amateur Division 1st Place Crisco Classic Cherry

Ingredients

CRUST

1 cup flour

½ cup unsweetened cocoa powder

⅓ cup sugar

¼ teaspoon salt

½ cup Crisco shortening

1 large egg yolk

3 to 4 tablespoons cold water

FILLING

½ cup plus 2 tablespoons sugar

¼ cup unsweetened cocoa powder

2 tablespoons cornstarch

2 cups heavy whipping cream

2 egg yolks

1½ oz. bittersweet chocolate

1½ oz. semi-sweet chocolate

1 tablespoon butter

1 teaspoon vanilla extract

TOPPING

(2) 15 oz. cans good-quality cherry
   pie filling

½ teaspoon almond extract

1 cup whipping cream

1 tablespoon powdered sugar

½ teaspoon vanilla extract

2 oz. milk chocolate bar (grated for
   garnish)

Directions

For the crust: Preheat oven to 425°F. Combine flour, cocoa powder, sugar, and salt. Blend in shortening with fingers until mixture resembles coarse meal. Add egg yolk and gently blend. Sprinkle cold water over ingredients until they are moist. Form into a ball and chill.

Roll dough between two sheets of waxed paper to 1/8 inch thickness. Place in pie tin. Dock bottom and sides of pastry shell by perforating dough with a fork. Use pie weights or dried beans to weigh down crust. Bake for 10–12 minutes. Remove from oven. Let cool to room temperature.

For the filling: Whisk together sugar, cocoa, and cornstarch in a saucepan over medium-high heat. Gradually whisk in heavy cream and egg yolks, stirring constantly until mixture is thick, about 2 to 4 minutes. Remove from heat. Add chocolates, butter, and vanilla. Whisk together until well-blended. Pour into pre-baked pie shell. Press plastic wrap directly on top of pie and refrigerate 4 hours or overnight.

For the topping: Pour cans of cherry pie filling into a colander to strain off excess liquid. Place strained cherries in bowl. Fold in almond extract. Gently spoon the cherries onto the top of the chocolate layer. Beat together whipping cream, powdered sugar, and vanilla. With a pastry bag, pipe cream onto the top of the cherry layer leaving a small pool in the center of the pie without any cream. Grate chocolate bar on top of whipped cream for garnish.

Sweet Tart Cherry Pie

Kathy Costello, Tallmadge, OH 2007 APC Crisco National Pie Championships Amateur Division 3rd Place Crisco Classic Cherry

Ingredients

CRUST
1 egg
1 teaspoon clear vanilla
2 tablespoons powdered sugar
1¼ cups butter-flavored Crisco shortening
2¾ cups plus 2 tablespoons flour
¼ cup ice water

FILLING
¼ cup sugar
½ cup powder sugar
¾ cup cherry juice (drained from cherries; use an equal amount of juice from each type of cherry; make up difference with water)
2½ cups canned tart cherries in water, drained
2½ cups canned sweet cherries in water, drained
⅛ teaspoon nutty amaretto oil flavoring.

DECORATIVE GARNISH
Leftover pie dough
Red and green food coloring
Cocoa

Directions

For the crust: Mix egg, vanilla, powdered sugar, and Crisco until creamy. Mix until all ingredients are incorporated. Do not over mix dough. Form 2 discs and wrap in plastic wrap. Chill for an hour.

Remove dough from refrigerator. Place dough on a lightly floured piece of plastic wrap, sprinkle with flour, and cover with another sheet of plastic. Roll out dough to fit pie dish, then line bottom of pie dish with dough.

For the filling: Preheat oven to 375°F. Whisk sugar, powdered sugar, and cherry juice together and cook over medium heat. Stir until mixture begins to thicken. Add drained cherries and nutty amaretto oil flavoring. Continue to cook until mixture becomes thick and clear. Remove from heat, set aside to completely cool. After filling is cooled, place prepared filling in the pie dish and then cover with the other half of prepared rolled-out pie dough. Place small slits in top of pie for steam to escape. Beat 1 egg white until foamy and brush top of pie. Sprinkle lightly with sugar. Before placing pie in oven, place aluminum foil around the crimped edges of the pie to prevent overbrowning. Spray inner side of foil with flour cooking spray to prevent sticking when removing foil.

For decorative garnish: Use small amount of leftover pie dough and add several drops of red food coloring; then make 3 or more small marble-size balls to place on top of pie. Mix small amount of cocoa into dough to make stems to place under each cherry.

Mix small amount of green food coloring, press dough out on counter and cut out leaves, or use leaf cutter. Place leaves on stems.

Bake pie on bottom rack for 10 minutes. Then move pie up to middle rack for 40 to 45 minutes. Remove foil 5 minutes before pie is done.

Tom's Cheery Cherry Berry Pie

Linda Hundt, DeWitt, MI 2009 APC Crisco Professional Cherry 1st Place Crisco Classic Cherry and Best of Show

Ingredients

CRUST

1½ cups flour

¼ teaspoon baking powder

½ teaspoon salt

1 teaspoon sugar

½ cup Crisco shortening

½ teaspoon real almond extract

1 teaspoon fresh-squeezed lemon juice

½ teaspoon orange zest

½ cup dried Michigan cherries

1½ cups frozen blueberries

FILLING

4½ cups Montmorency tart cherries (frozen)

1 cup sugar

¼ cup cornstarch

CRUMB TOPPING

1 cup sugar

1 cup all-purpose flour

¼ teaspoon salt

1 stick butter, softened

Directions

For the crust: Mix all ingredients in a stand mixer on medium speed swiftly until dough texture appears "pea-like." Carefully sprinkle ice cold water in crust mix until it just starts to be fully moistened and gathers together. Pat into disc; wrap and refrigerate for at least one half hour. Roll out on floured surface and make and crimp piecrust. Freeze until ready to use.

For the filling: Preheat oven to 400°F. Combine frozen cherries, dried cherries, sugar, and cornstarch. Stir constantly on medium-high heat until boiling. Boil for one minute or until thickened. Add almond extract, lemon juice, and zest. Pour blueberries on bottom pie shell and pour cherry mixture over them.

For the topping: Mix together all crumb topping ingredients by hand or with a pastry blender until crumbly. Cover filling with crumb topping. Bake for 45 minutes to one hour or until filling is bubbling over crust.

I'm So Cheery Cherry Pie

Susan Boyle, DeBary, FL 2011 APC Crisco National Pie Championships
Professional Division 1ˢᵗ Place Crisco Classic Cherry

Ingredients

CRUST

2 cups all-purpose flour	1 teaspoon salt
¾ cup Crisco	6 tablespoons ice-cold water

FILLING

5 cups tart cherries	½ teaspoon cinnamon
½ cup dried cherries	$1/3$ cup cornstarch
½ cup cherry juice concentrate	4 drops red food coloring
¼ teaspoon almond extract	

Directions

For the crust: Mix flour and salt in bowl. Add Crisco, and then use a pastry blender to cut in butter. Slowly add water one tablespoon at a time until mixture forms ball. Divide dough and place on floured surface. Shape like a pancake and roll out to fit upside-down pie plate. Fold into quarters and place in pie plate. Trim dough to ½ inch over edge of plate and flute. Refrigerate other half of dough for leaf designs to place on top of filling.

For the filling: Preheat oven to 425°F. Soak dried cherries in cherry juice about fifteen minutes. Do not drain. Add 5 cups of tart cherries, sugar, cornstarch, cinnamon, almond extract, and food coloring. Toss gently so as not to break cherries and to coat well. Add filling to an unbaked pastry shell and flute. Cut leaf designs and lay on top of filling.

Bake at 425°F for 10 minutes, then reduce heat to 375°F for 50 minutes.

Blue Ridge Cherry Pie

Emily Spaugh, Yadkinville, NC 2010 APC Crisco National Pie Championships Amateur Division 1ˢᵗ Place Crisco Classic Cherry

Ingredients

CRUST

3 cups all-purpose flour

1 tablespoon plus 1 or 1½ teaspoons sugar

1 teaspoon salt

1 cup plus 2 tablespoons Crisco shortening

½ cup ice water

1 egg slightly beaten

1 tablespoon vinegar

FILLING

1 cup cherry juice

1 cup sugar

¼ cup cornstarch

4 cups pitted red cherries

2 tablespoons butter

½ teaspoon almond extract

½ teaspoon vanilla

1 or 2 drops red food coloring

GLAZE

Brush with milk, sprinkle with sugar.

Directions

For the crust: Combine flour, 1 tablespoon plus 1 to 1 ½ teaspoons sugar and salt in large bowl. Cut in Crisco until all flour is blended to form pea-size chunks. Combine water, egg, and vinegar in small bowl. Sprinkle over flour mixture, 1 tablespoon at a time. Toss lightly with fork until dough forms a ball (you may not use all liquid). Divide dough into pieces. Flatten each piece and wrap in plastic. Refrigerate until chilled.

For the filling: Preheat oven to 375°F. In saucepan, combine cherry juice, sugar, and cornstarch. Cook until mixture begins to thicken, but it need not boil. Allow to cool slightly. Add cherries and flavoring. Roll bottom crust and place in 9-inch pie plate. Roll out top crust and cut into strips to form a lattice top. Spoon filling into pastry-lined pie pan. Dot with butter and top with lattice crust. Brush with milk and sprinkle with sugar. Bake 35 to 40 minutes or until filling in center is bubbly and crust is golden brown. Serve barely warm or at room temperature.

Mixed Berry

KP's Berry Pie

Karen Panosian, Celebration, FL 2005 APC Crisco National Pie Championships Amateur Division 2nd Place Celebration

Ingredients

CRUST
2 cups all-purpose flour
½ teaspoon salt
²/₃ cup Crisco shortening
1 teaspoon vanilla extract
6 tablespoons cold water

LAYER 1
1¼ cups crushed graham crackers and chopped walnuts, mixed
¹/₃ cup butter
¼ cup sugar

FILLING
1¼ cups fresh blueberries

1¼ cups fresh raspberries
1¼ cups fresh blackberries
1¼ cups fresh strawberries
¾ cup sugar
¹/₃ cup all-purpose flour
¹/₈ teaspoon cinnamon
¹/₈ teaspoon ginger
¹/₈ teaspoon nutmeg
¹/₈ teaspoon allspice
½ cup coconut
Butter for dotting

GLAZE
¼ cup milk
Sugar for sprinkling

Directions

For the crust: Combine flour and salt. Cut in shortening until texture resembles coarse meal. Mix water and vanilla. Add water mixture 1 tablespoon at a time until crust comes together. Form into a ball. Divide in two. Roll out one half to line the bottom of a 9-inch pie dish. Roll out the other for a top crust.

For layer 1: Preheat oven to 375°F. Combine ingredients and press into the bottom crust.

For the filling: Combine fruit, sugar, flour, spices, and coconut in a large bowl. Coat well. Pour into pie crust. Dot the fruit filling with butter.

For the glaze: Place top crust on pie. Brush the crust with milk and sprinkle with sugar. Cut vents as appropriate. Bake pie at 375°F for 50 minutes.

Bumbleberry Pie

Hunny Lee, Kokomo, IN 2010 APC Crisco National Pie Championships Amateur Division 1ˢᵗ Place Fruit/Berry

Ingredients

CRUST

1 cup butter-flavored shortening

3 tablespoons sugar

2 cups flour

½ cup cold water

FILLING

1 cup black raspberries

1 cup red raspberries

1 cup rhubarb

2 cups apples

$1/3$ cup flour

1 $1/3$ cups sugar

4 tablespoons butter

Directions

For the crust: Mix shortening, flour, and sugar together until dough forms pea-size balls. Add water and gather dough into a ball (makes 2 single crusts). Roll out and place one crust in pie dish.

For the filling: Preheat oven to 350°F. Mix all fruit in a bowl. Add sugar and mix well. Then add flour to thicken. Add butter and mix again. Pour into pie crust. Roll out top crust. Cut dough into ½ inch wide strips. Weave strips in a lattice design over filling. Trim strips even with the bottom crust. Moisten strips with water and fold under with bottom crust. Crimp. Bake for 1 hour or until done.

Blueberry–Raspberry Pie

Raquel Hammond, St. Cloud, FL 2005 APC Crisco National Pie Championships Amateur Division 1ˢᵗ Place Fruit/Berry

Ingredients

CRUST
2 cups unbleached flour
1 cup cake flour
1½ tablespoons sugar
1 teaspoon salt
8 tablespoons (1 stick) frozen
    unsalted butter, cut up
½ cup plus 2 tablespoons frozen
    Crisco shortening, cut up
2 tablespoons vinegar
1 large egg yolk
4 to 5 tablespoons ice water, or as
    needed
¼ cup crushed cornflakes

EGG GLAZE
1 large egg white with 1 tablespoon
    water added

¼ cup blueberry preserves

FILLING
2 cups fresh blueberries or (2) 15 oz.
    cans blueberries, drained (plump
    only)
2 cups frozen blueberries, partially
    thawed
4 cups frozen raspberries, partially
    thawed
¾ cup sugar
3½ tablespoons quick cooking
    tapioca
Big pinch of salt
¾ tablespoon cinnamon
¼ teaspoon nutmeg
1 tablespoon lemon juice
2 tablespoons unsalted butter, cut up

Directions

For the crust: Blend together dry ingredients in large bowl. Add the butter and shortening. Using a pastry blender, cut in fat until mixture resembles dry rice. Add egg yolk, vinegar, and a minimum amount of water. Lightly toss until mixture just begins to clump together. If dough looks too dry, sprinkle on a little more water. Dough should cling together and feel pliable, but not sticky.

Form dough into a cohesive ball on a piece of waxed paper by lifting opposite corners of paper and pressing them together. Flatten into 6-inch disk for single shell, or divide in half and make two discs for double-crust pie. Wrap dough in plastic wrap and refrigerate for at least 1 hour or even overnight (the longer the better). Soften dough at room temperature for a few minutes before rolling out. When ready, roll out bottom crust and line 9-inch pie plate. Roll out top crust. Refrigerate both for 15 minutes.

For the filling: Preheat oven to 425°F. In a large bowl, combine berries. In another bowl, combine sugar, tapioca, salt, cinnamon, and nutmeg. Sprinkle over berries, add lemon juice, and gently stir together. Brush egg glaze on bottom of pastry shell, then spread ¼ cup of blueberry preserves on bottom as well. Pour filling into pie shell and dot with butter. Attach top crust either as a whole or in pastry cutouts. If using a whole top crust, poke holes for steam to vent. Brush with egg glaze and sprinkle with sugar.

Bake at 425°F in lower third of oven for 15 minutes. Raise rack to center, lower temperature to 350°F, and then bake an additional 50 to 55 minutes. Half-way through baking time, cover with foil if browning too much.

Transfer to wire rack and cool for at least 2 hours or longer. Slice and serve. Refrigerate leftovers covered with loosely tented foil.

Fruity Fruit Pie

Caroline Imig, Oconto, WI 2011 APC Crisco National Pie Championships Professional Division 1ˢᵗ Place Fruit/Berry

Ingredients

CRUST
1½ cups flour
1 tablespoon sugar
½ tablespoon salt
½ cup cold Crisco shortening
¼ cup cold water

FILLING
1½ cups white chocolate chips
¼ cup evaporated milk
8 oz. package cream cheese, softened
1 tablespoon strawberry extract
2 drops red food coloring

FRUIT TOPPING
½ cup blueberries
3 cups sliced strawberries
4 sliced kiwis
1 cup raspberries
Whipped cream

Directions

For the crust: Preheat oven to 375°F. Combine dry ingredients. Cut cold shortening into flour mixture until particles are the size of small peas. Sprinkle in water, tossing with fork until all flour is moistened and pastry can be formed into ball. When ready, roll out pie crust and place in pie pan. Spread foil out on pie crust and fill with pie weights. Bake for 8 to 10 minutes or until golden brown.

For the filling: In microwave-safe bowl, place white chocolate chips and evaporated milk. Microwave 1 minute. Stir. If necessary, microwave an additional 15 seconds, stirring until chips are melted. Beat in cream cheese, strawberry extract, and red food coloring. Spread on bottom of baked pie shell.

For the topping: Arrange fruit in decorative pattern on top of filling. Garnish with whipped cream.

Rhubarb–Strawberry–Raspberry Pie

Susan Gills, Boulder, CO 1998 APC Crisco National Pie Championships Amateur Division 1ˢᵗ Place Fruit/Berry and Best of Show

Ingredients

CRUST

²/₃ cup shortening

2 tablespoons butter

1 teaspoon salt

2 cups flour

4 tablespoons ice-cold water

Sugar for sprinkling

FILLING

1 cup strawberries, cut in half or in quarters

1 cup raspberries

2 cups rhubarb, cut into ½ inch pieces

¾ cup sugar

¹/₃ cup flour

1 tablespoon butter, melted

1 teaspoon lemon juice

Directions

For the crust: Mix flour and salt. Add shortening and butter, and mix until texture is like coarse cornmeal. Add water and form dough into a ball. Let sit at least 20 minutes before rolling out. Divide in half. Roll out bottom crust and place in pie pan.

For the filling: Mix sugar and flour. Add to fruits. Refrigerate overnight. Just before adding fruit to pastry-lined pie pan, add melted butter and lemon juice to fruit mixture.

Preheat oven to 400°F. Pour filling into pie shell. Roll out top crust and place on top. Crimp edges and sprinkle lightly with sugar. Bake at 400°F for 10 minutes, then turn the temperature down to 350°F. Bake for 40 to 50 minutes until crust is golden brown.

Sunshine Pie

Melissa Mace, Celebration, FL 2002 APC Crisco National Pie Championships Amateur Division 2nd Place Celebration

Ingredients

CRUST

1¾ cups flour	2 tablespoons Crisco
1 teaspoon salt	5 tablespoons ice water
10 tablespoons butter	

FILLING

2 Florida oranges	2 tablespoons cornstarch
1 Florida lemon	4 eggs
2 cups sugar	4 tablespoons melted butter
¼ teaspoon salt	

Directions

For the crust: Combine flour and salt. Cut butter and Crisco into flour and salt until it looks like coarse meal. Add up to 5 tablespoons water. Form into a loose ball. Knead several times on a lightly floured surface. Divide into two balls and refrigerate for 30 minutes. Roll crusts out between two lightly floured pieces of plastic wrap

For the filling: Preheat oven to 425°F. Grate orange and lemon zest into a bowl. Thinly slice oranges into quarter rounds. Discard ends and seeds. Gently toss with zest. Add sugar and salt. Cover and leave at room temperature for 24 hours. Juice lemon. Dissolve cornstarch in lemon juice and lemon pulp. Whisk eggs until frothy. Add lemon juice mixture and butter. Stir in oranges.

Place bottom crust in pie plate. Pour in orange mixture. Cover with top crust. Fold and crimp edges. Brush with water and sprinkle with sugar. Cut vent holes in top crust. Bake for 25 minutes. Turn oven down to 350°F and bake for an additional 25 to 30 minutes.

Deep-Dish Deluxe Banana Split Pie

Carol Socier, Bay City, MI 2011 APC Crisco National Pie Championships Amateur Division 1st Place Open

Ingredients

CRUST

1½ cups all-purpose flour

⅓ cup crushed vanilla wafers

1 teaspoon sugar

½ cup Crisco shortening

5 to 6 tablespoons cold water

FILLING

½ cup chocolate fudge ice cream topping

¼ cup plus 2 tablespoons sugar

2 tablespoons cornstarch

¼ teaspoon salt

¾ cup water

½ 3 oz. package strawberry Jell-O

10 oz. package frozen strawberries

3 large bananas

3 oz. package French vanilla instant pudding

1 ¾ cups half and half

1 cup whipped cream

1½ cups miniature marshmallows

GARNISH

Whipped cream

Maraschino cherries

Chopped peanuts

Chocolate Magic Shell ice cream topping

Directions

For the crust: Preheat oven to 400°F. Combine flour, wafers, and sugar in large bowl. Cut in shortening with pastry blender until pea-size pieces form. Add water, 1 tablespoon at a time, tossing with a fork until dough forms a ball. On lightly floured surface, roll out dough to fit 9-inch deep-dish pie plate. Flute edges, and prick bottom and sides with a fork. Bake for 12 to 15 minutes or until golden brown. Cool for at least 1 hour before filling.

For the filling: Drizzle chocolate fudge ice cream topping on bottom pie crust and refrigerate. Combine sugar, cornstarch, salt, and water in a saucepan. Cook over medium heat until thick and clear. Add strawberry Jell-O, stirring until dissolved. Add frozen strawberries. Place in refrigerator until cool and thick. Assemble pie by slicing bananas over fudge topping. Gently spoon strawberry mixture over bananas. Put in refrigerator until set. Meanwhile, prepare instant French vanilla pudding according to package directions, using half and half. Fold in whipped cream and marshmallows. Spread over strawberry layer.

Garnish with more whipped cream, cherries, and chopped peanuts. Drizzle with Magic Shell. Keep refrigerated.

Back to the Islands Pie

Janet Ropp, Edgewater, FL 2008 APC Crisco National Pie Championships Amateur Division 1st Place Open

Ingredients

CRUST

2 cups graham cracker crumbs

½ cup butter, melted

3 tablespoons sugar

2 tablespoons vanilla flavoring

FILLING

8 oz. package cream cheese, softened

3.4 oz. package instant vanilla pudding

2½ cups milk

²/₃ cup coconut

FRUIT LAYER

2 bananas, sliced

1 cup chopped mango, fresh or frozen

8 oz. can crushed pineapple, drained

TOPPING

8 oz. frozen whipped topping, thawed

¼ teaspoon coconut flavoring

¹/₃ cup chopped macadamia nuts

Directions

For the crust: Preheat oven to 350°F. Melt butter and add to rest of crust ingredients. Press into 9 ½-inch glass pie plate and bake for 10 minutes. Let crust cool before adding filling.

For the filling: Beat together cream cheese and milk. Add instant vanilla pudding and beat well for about 2 minutes. Add coconut and blend well.

For the fruit layer: Place sliced bananas over crust. Cover with pudding mixture. Drain pineapple and mix with chopped mango. Sprinkle mango and pineapple over pudding mixture.

For the topping: Mix together frozen whipped topping and coconut flavoring. Spread over pie. Sprinkle with chopped macadamia nuts. Chill and serve.

Cherry Red Raspberry Pie

Phyllis Bartholomew, Columbus, NE 2004 APC Crisco National Pie Championships Amateur Division 1st Place Fruit/Berry and Best of Show

Ingredients

CRUST

2 cups flour

1 cup cake flour

1 cup Crisco shortening, butter-
   flavored

1 whole egg

1 tablespoon cider vinegar

½ teaspoon salt

⅓ cup ice water

FILLING

10 oz. package frozen red raspberries

2 cups canned sour pitted cherries,
   drained

1 cup sugar

3 tablespoons cornstarch

2 tablespoons butter

¼ teaspoon salt

Milk and sugar (to top the crust)

Directions

For the crust: Mix the flours and butter powder and cut in the shortening until it resembles coarse crumbs. Beat together the other ingredients and stir into the flour. Mix just until it is incorporated. Form into a disc, wrap in plastic wrap, and chill. Roll out about ⅓ of the dough between 2 sheets of wax paper and line pie dish.

For the filling: Preheat oven to 350°F. Thaw frozen raspberries, saving the juice, and add enough of the juice from the cherries to make 1 cup liquid. In a saucepan, mix sugar, cornstarch, and salt. Stir in one cup of juice. Add cherries and cook over medium heat until thick and clear. Cook one more minute. Remove from heat and very gently fold in raspberries. Pour into pastry-lined pie dish. Add top crust. Seal edges, moisten top with hot milk, and sprinkle with sugar. Cut seam vents. Bake for about 45 minutes. This pie is extra pretty with a lattice top.

Peach

Ginger, You're a Peach Pie

John Sunvold, Winter Springs, FL 2009 APC Crisco National Pie Championships Amateur Division Fruit/Berry

Ingredients

CRUST

1¼ cups ginger cookies/snaps crumbs, processed in food processor

¼ cup sugar

3 tablespoons butter, melted

CREAM LAYER

1/3 cup cream cheese, softened

1/3 cup powdered sugar

5 oz. Cool Whip

PEACH LAYER

4 to 6 fresh peaches (canned will work if no fresh peaches are available; allow 7 canned peach slices for each fresh peach)

½ cup water

¼ teaspoon cinnamon

2/3 cup brown sugar

3 tablespoons cornstarch

1 tablespoon butter

Whipped topping and ginger cookies (optional garnish)

Directions

For the crust: Preheat oven to 375°F. Mix all ingredients together and press mixture into a 9-inch pie plate. Bake for 8 to 10 minutes. Allow to cool to room temperature. Place in refrigerator to cool completely.

For the cream layer: Mix together softened cream and powdered sugar. Fold in thawed Cool Whip. Spread onto ginger crumb crust. Refrigerate for 2 hours.

For the peach layer: Peel peaches and remove stones. Slice peaches into around 6 to 8 slices per peach. Pat peaches dry and place on a drying rack. Take the four worst-looking slices and chop them into very small, marble-sized pieces. In small saucepan, mix water, brown sugar, cinnamon, cornstarch, and butter. Stir constantly over medium heat. Bring to a boil, then add the chopped peach pieces. Simmer for up to 5 minutes or until thick. Cool.

Arrange fresh peach slices on top of cream layer so they cover top. Leave around ¼ inch of the cream layer showing all around. Pour the cooled brown sugar mixture over the peaches. Refrigerate 2 hours. Garnish with whipped topping and ginger cookies (optional).

Peaches and Creamy Cranberry Pie

Lisa Schiessl, Fond du Lac, WI 2009 APC Crisco National Pie Championships Amateur Division 3rd Place Open

Ingredients

CRUST
¾ cup all-purpose flour
½ tablespoon sugar
Pinch salt
½ cup Crisco
¼ cup cake flour
1 tablespoon liquid egg substitute
½ tablespoon vinegar
Water (to equal ¼ cup liquid)

FILLING
½ cup sour cream
½ cup mascarpone cheese
8 oz. cream cheese
1 egg
2 tablespoons flour

1 teaspoon vanilla
2 tablespoons peach jam
¾ cup sugar
1 teaspoon cinnamon
1 teaspoon nutmeg
2 cups diced peaches (frozen or fresh)
1 cup whole cranberries
1 cup crushed cranberries

TOPPING
¾ cup crushed coconut macaroons
¼ cup brown sugar
½ teaspoon cinnamon
1 tablespoon flour
¼ cup butter (melted)

Directions

For the crust: In medium-sized bowl, whisk together all-purpose flour, sugar, and salt. With a pastry blender, cut in Crisco until pieces of dough resemble coarse crumbs. Sift cake flour over crumbs and mix lightly with fork. In separate small bowl, whisk together liquid egg, vinegar, and enough water to equal ¼ cup liquid. Stir egg mixture into flour mixture just until moistened. Roll dough into large ball. On a lightly floured board, roll out ball of dough to fit a 9-inch pie plate. Transfer prepared dough to pie plate; trim and flute.

For the filling: Preheat oven to 400°F. In large mixing bowl, cream together sour cream, mascarpone cheese, cream cheese, egg, flour, vanilla, peach jam, sugar, cinnamon, and nutmeg. Mix until well-blended. Add diced peaches, whole cranberries, and crushed cranberries. Stir to coat. Pour into prepared bottom pie crust. Bake pie for 10 minutes, then reduce oven to 350°F and bake for 25 to 30 minutes.

For the topping: While pie is baking, in small mixing bowl combine crushed coconut macaroons, brown sugar, cinnamon, and flour. Pour melted butter evenly over combined topping ingredients. Set aside for 5 minutes, then, using your fingertips, break the mixture into ¼- to ½-inch crumbs. Top pie with coconut macaroon topping and bake 10 to 15 more minutes at 350°F.

Pumpkin

Harvest Pumpkin Pie

Amy Freeze, Sebring, FL 2011 APC Crisco National Pie Championships Amateur Division 2nd Place Pumpkin

Ingredients

CRUST

¼ cup butter

¼ cup shortening

1¼ cups all-purpose flour

1 tablespoon sugar

¼ teaspoon salt

1 egg yolk

2 tablespoons ice water

½ teaspoon vinegar

FILLING

15 oz. can pumpkin

14 oz. can sweetened condensed milk

4 eggs

1 cup apple butter

1 teaspoon cinnamon

½ teaspoon ground ginger

½ teaspoon nutmeg

½ teaspoon salt

1 teaspoon vanilla extract

1 cup chopped candied pecans

TOPPING

8 oz. Cool Whip

1/8 teaspoon nutmeg

¼ teaspoon ground ginger

½ teaspoon cinnamon

1 teaspoon clear vanilla

Directions

For the crust: Beat together butter and shortening until smooth and creamy. Chill until firm. Sift together flour, sugar, and salt in medium bowl. Using a fork, cut butter and shortening into dry ingredients until mixture has a coarse crumb texture. Mix egg yolk, ice water, and vinegar into dough, then form into ball and refrigerate at least 1 hour. Roll out on floured surface, place in pan, crimp edges, and fill.

For the filling: Preheat oven to 425°F. In a large bowl, whisk pumpkin, condensed milk, eggs, apple butter, spices, vanilla, and salt until smooth. Pour into prepared crust. Bake at 425°F for 10 minutes. Reduce heat and bake at 350°F for 20 minutes. Sprinkle with chopped pecans and continue baking for 15 minutes or until knife inserted in center comes out clean. Cool completely before refrigerating.

For the topping: Gently fold together all ingredients. Pipe rosettes around edge of pie before serving.

Walnut Crunch Pumpkin Pie

Christine Montalvo, Windsor Heights, IA 2005 APC Crisco National Pie Championships Amateur Division 1ˢᵗ Place Pumpkin

Ingredients

CRUST

2 ½ cups all-purpose flour

½ teaspoon salt

1 ½ sticks (³/₄ cup) cold unsalted
    butter

¼ cup cold Crisco shortening

4 to 6 tablespoons ice water

FILLING

²/₃ cup golden brown sugar, packed

½ cup sugar

2 tablespoons all-purpose flour

½ teaspoon salt

½ teaspoon ground cinnamon

¹/₈ teaspoon ground allspice

¹/₈ teaspoon ground cloves

¹/₈ teaspoon ground ginger

1½ cups canned solid-packed
    pumpkin

2 tablespoons mild-flavored (light)
    molasses

3 large eggs

1 cup whipping cream

TOPPING

4 tablespoons butter

1 cup chopped walnuts

¾ cup packed brown sugar

1 cup whipping cream plus 3 table-
    spoons powdered sugar

Directions

For the crust: In a food processor, add flour and salt. Pulse to mix. Add cold butter and Crisco, which have been cut into small pieces. Pulse 6 to 8 times until mixture resembles coarse meal with some small pea-size butter lumps. Drizzle 4 tablespoons ice water evenly over mixture and pulse 3 to 4 times more until dough holds together. Add more water, 1 tablespoon at a time, until dough holds together. Form into 2 balls, and then flatten each into a disc. Wrap discs separately in plastic wrap and refrigerate at least 1 hour.

Divide dough into 2 pieces. On a lightly floured surface with a lightly floured rolling pin, roll out one piece of dough into a 10-inch round (about

1/8 inch thick). Fit a 9-inch pie plate with one piece of dough and flute edges. Reserve 2nd piece of dough for another time. Refrigerate (or freeze) while preparing filling.

For the filling: Place baking sheet in oven and preheat to 450°F. Whisk brown sugar, sugar, flour, salt, cinnamon, allspice, cloves, and ginger together in large bowl to blend. Whisk in pumpkin, molasses, eggs, and whipping cream. Pour mixture into frozen crust. Place pie on preheated baking sheet in oven. Bake 10 minutes. Reduce heat to 325°F and bake until sides puff and center is just set, about 40 minutes. Cool completely. Preheat broiler. Prepare Walnut Crunch topping.

For the walnut crunch topping: In a small saucepan, over low heat, melt butter. Stir in walnuts and brown sugar and mix until thoroughly combined. Spoon evenly over pie. Broil pie 3 minutes, 5 to 7 inches from broiler, or until topping is golden and sugar dissolves. Cool pie again on wire rack.

In a small bowl, beat heavy whipping cream and powdered sugar with electric mixer until stiff peaks form. Pipe around edge of cooled pie.

Pecan Maple Streusel Pumpkin Pie

Jennifer Nystrom, Morrow, OH 2008 APC Crisco National Pie Championships Amateur Division 2nd Place Pumpkin

Ingredients

CRUST

2 ¾ cups all-purpose flour

1 teaspoon table salt

¾ cup vegetable shortening

½ cup butter (not margarine)

1 egg, slightly beaten

¹/₃ cup cold buttermilk

FILLING

2 eggs, slightly beaten

15 oz. canned pumpkin

14 oz. canned sweetened condensed
   milk

1 teaspoon cinnamon

½ teaspoon ground ginger

½ teaspoon ground nutmeg

¹/₈ teaspoon ground cloves

TOPPING

¼ cup packed light brown sugar

3 tablespoons flour

½ teaspoon cinnamon

2 tablespoons cold butter

½ cup chopped pecans

MAPLE DRIZZLE GARNISH

1 cup confectioner's sugar

3 tablespoons whipping cream

½ teaspoon Mapleine

Directions

    For the crust: In a large bowl, mix together the flour and the salt. With a pastry blender, cut in shortening until flour resembles cornmeal. Cut in butter until it resembles small peas. In a small bowl, beat egg with a fork. Beat in buttermilk. Mixture will look almost gelatinous. Quickly mix buttermilk mixture in with the flour until flour just begins to hold together. Separate flour mixture into halves and form each half into a disc. Wrap each disc tightly with plastic wrap and refrigerate for at least an hour and up to two days.

    After the dough has chilled, preheat oven to 375°F and remove one disc from refrigerator (save second disc for another use). On a lightly floured surface, roll out disc to fit a 9-inch pie pan. Place a piece of parchment paper inside pie pan over the crust and fill with pie weights. Bake for 20 minutes or until almost done and just beginning to turn lightly brown. Remove from oven and remove parchment paper and pie weights. Set aside to cool slightly.

For the filling: While crust is cooling, preheat oven to 425°F. In a medium bowl that allows for easy pouring, slightly beat eggs. Whisk in pumpkin and sweetened condensed milk. Whisk in cinnamon, ginger, nutmeg, and cloves until well combined. Set aside.

To make the streusel topping: In a medium-sized bowl, mix brown sugar, flour, and cinnamon. Cut in butter until it resembles small peas. Mix in pecans.

Pour pumpkin mixture into baked crust. Top evenly with streusel mixture, making sure to put it on very lightly so as not to mix it in with the pumpkin. Bake in a 425°F oven for 15 minutes. Reduce heat to 350°F and bake for an additional 45 minutes or until a knife inserted in the center comes out clean. Place foil around the edges so as not to burn the crust.

Remove the pie from the oven and let cool completely. When completely cooled, make maple drizzle by thoroughly mixing the confectioner's sugar, whipping cream, and Mapleine in a small bowl with a spoon. Drizzle glaze over cooled pie. Refrigerate at least two hours before serving.

Real Pumpkin Pie

Jill Jones, Palm Bay, FL 2009 APC Crisco National Pie Championships Amateur Division 1ˢᵗ Place Pumpkin

Ingredients

CRUST

1 cup flour

½ teaspoon salt

¼ tablespoon sugar

½ cup shortening

1 egg

1 ½ tablespoons water (ice-cold)

¼ tablespoon vinegar

FILLING

1 small cooking pumpkin (4 to 6 inches)

¾ cup sugar

½ teaspoon salt

1 teaspoon cinnamon

¾ teaspoon pumpkin pie spice

1 smidgen fresh ground nutmeg

¼ teaspoon pure vanilla

2 eggs

14 oz. can sweetened condensed milk

Directions

For the crust: Mix flour, salt, and sugar, then cut in shortening with fork or pastry cutter until crumbly. Add egg, water, and vinegar. Scrape out of bowl onto floured surface. Roll into ball, wrap in plastic wrap, and refrigerate ½ to 1 hour. Roll dough out on a floured surface and place in pie pan.

For the filling: Preheat oven to 425°F. Cut pumpkin in half, and scrape out seeds and string membranes of pumpkin. Quarter pumpkin. In a double steamer, steam pumpkin until soft and skin peels off by touch (45 minutes to 1 hour). Mash with potato masher, then squeeze water out of mashed pumpkin through cheesecloth. Combine pumpkin, sugar, salt, cinnamon, pumpkin pie spice, nutmeg, and vanilla, and mix well. Add eggs and milk. Mix well. Pour into unbaked pie crust. Bake for 15 minutes. Reduce heat to 350°F and cover crust edge. Bake for 40 to 50 minutes. Let cool 3 hours before serving. Refrigerate.

Honey Crunch Pumpkin Pie

Phyllis Bartholomew, Columbus, NE 2003 APC Crisco National Pie Championships Amateur Division 2nd Place Pumpkin

Ingredients

CRUST

2 cups flour

1 cup cake flour

1 cup Crisco shortening

2 tablespoons powdered butter
   flavoring

½ teaspoon salt

½ to 1 teaspoon pumpkin pie spice

1 egg

1 tablespoon cider vinegar

⅓ cup ice water

FILLING

1 cup brown sugar

1 tablespoon cornstarch

2 teaspoons cinnamon

¾ teaspoon ground ginger

¼ teaspoon salt

(1) 16 oz. can of solid-packed
   pumpkin

¾ cup whipping cream

½ cup sour cream

3 large eggs, beaten

HONEY CRUNCH TOPPING

¼ cup packed brown sugar

2 tablespoons honey

2 tablespoons butter

¾ cup chopped nuts (pecans are best)

WHIPPED CREAM TOPPING

1 cup heavy whipping cream

3 tablespoons powdered sugar

1 teaspoon unflavored gelatin

2 tablespoons cold water

Directions

For the crust: Mix all the dry ingredients together and cut in the shortening to resemble coarse crumbs. Beat the rest of the ingredients together and add to flour. Stir only until incorporated. Wrap in plastic and chill for several hours. Roll out and line pie dish.

For the filling: Preheat oven to 400°F. Mix together brown sugar, cornstarch, cinnamon, ground ginger, and salt so there are no lumps. Then add the rest of the ingredients. Stir well to blend. Pour into a 9- or 10-inch pastry-lined pie dish and bake at 400°F on the bottom rack for 10 minutes. Reduce the temperature to 350°F, move to the middle rack, and bake for an additional 50 minutes, just until set in the middle. Remove from the oven and cool on a rack.

For the honey crunch topping: Cook sugar, honey, and butter in a small pan until the sugar is dissolved, about 2 minutes. Add the nuts and let cool. When cool, add to the middle two thirds of the pie.

For the whipped cream topping: Sprinkle gelatin over the water and let set for several minutes. Set over low heat until melted. Whip the cream to soft peaks and add the gelatin and sugar. Beat to stiff peaks. Pipe a decorative ribbon of whipped cream around the pie between the crust and the nut mixture.

Octoberfest Pie

Raine Gottess, Coconut Creek, FL 2008 APC Crisco National Pie Championships Amateur Division 1st Place Pumpkin

Ingredients

CRUST

18 whole Keebler cinnamon graham crackers

½ cup butter

4 tablespoons sugar

FILLING—LAYER ONE

8 oz. package Philadelphia Cream Cheese, softened

¹/₈ cup sour cream

1 small egg

¼ cup sugar

½ teaspoon vanilla

1 tablespoon flour

FILLING—LAYER TWO

8 oz. package Philadelphia Cream Cheese, softened

1 teaspoon vanilla

1½ cups powdered sugar

½ cup canned plain pumpkin

¼ teaspoon cinnamon

¼ teaspoon ginger

¹/₈ teaspoon cloves

8 oz. Cool Whip topping

FILLING—LAYER THREE

4 oz. Jell-O cheesecake flavored pudding mix

½ cup milk

¾ cup plain canned pumpkin

¼ teaspoon ginger

¼ teaspoon cinnamon

¹/₈ teaspoon nutmeg

¹/₈ teaspoon cloves

1 cup Cool Whip topping

Directions

For the crust: Using a food processor, finely crumble the graham crackers. Add sugar, and then place in a bowl. Toss in melted butter until moistened. Using the back of a large spoon, press mixture into a 10-inch deep-dish pie pan to form a crust. Freeze.

For layer 1: Preheat oven to 450°F. Using a mixer, beat well the softened cream cheese, sugar, and egg. Add in sour cream, flour, and vanilla. Pour into graham cracker crust. Cover the edges with foil. Bake as follows without opening the oven door: In a 450°F oven, bake for 8 minutes. Decrease oven temperature to 250°F and continue baking for another 20 minutes. Turn off oven, and leave in oven for 15 minutes. Cool on a wire rack.

For layer 2: Using a mixer, beat softened cream cheese with vanilla. Add powdered sugar. Mix in pumpkin and spices. Fold in Cool Whip. Spread over cooled pie. Freeze.

For layer 3: In a bowl, using a wire whisk, toss pudding and milk until thickened. Add in pumpkin and spices. Fold in Cool Whip. Spread over layer 2. Refrigerate about 6 hours until firm.

Tasty Pumpkin Pie

Sarah Spaugh, Winston-Salem, NC 2005 APG Crisco National Pie
Championships Amateur Division 3 Place Pumpkin

Ingredients

CRUST
2 cups flour
1 teaspoon salt
2/3 cup Crisco shortening
5 to 6 tablespoons cold water
1 tablespoon vinegar

FILLING
3 large eggs
2 cups fresh pumpkin, mashed, or
    15-oz. can solid-packed pumpkin
½ cup granulated sugar
¼ cup firmly packed dark brown
    sugar
¼ cup 100% amber maple syrup

1 teaspoon allspice
½ teaspoon cinnamon
1/8 teaspoon ground cloves
½ cup milk
¼ cup light cream

MAPLE LEAVES TOPPING
Cut out maple leaves or small pump-
    kins from crust scraps

WHIPPED CREAM TOPPING
  (OPTIONAL)
1 cup whipping cream
4 tablespoons pulverized sugar
½ teaspoon vanilla

Directions

For the crust: Combine the flour and the salt. Cut the shortening into the flour, then combine the water and vinegar. Gradually add the vinegar mixture into the flour until dough just holds together. Form into a ball, roll out, and place into a 9-inch pie pan.

For the filling: Preheat oven to 350°F. Beat the eggs lightly with a whisk in a large bowl. Stir in the pumpkin. Combine the sugar and spices. Stir in the maple syrup. Slowly stir in the milk and cream. Pour into a 9-inch pie shell. Bake for about 45 minutes or until the center is set.

For the maple leaves topping: Cut out maple leaves or small pumpkins from crust scraps. Bake 10–12 minutes or until golden brown and place on pie before serving.

For the optional whipped cream topping: Combine ingredients and whip until stiff. Put on top of pie before serving.

Farm-fresh Pumpkin Pie with Pecan Topping

Tricia Largay, Brewer, ME 2011 APC Crisco National Pie Championships Amateur Division 3rd Place Pumpkin

Ingredients

CRUST
⅓ cup plus 2 tablespoons Crisco butter-flavored shortening
1 cup all-purpose flour
¼ teaspoon salt
Pinch of sugar
6 to 7 tablespoons ice-cold water

½ cup sugar
1 tablespoon brown sugar
½ teaspoon pumpkin pie spice
1 tablespoon molasses
2 large eggs
Pinch of ground cloves
⅓ cup evaporated milk

FILLING
2 cans pure pumpkin (fresh pumpkins when in season cooked fork tender)
4 tablespoons melted butter

TOPPING
¾ cup brown sugar
⅓ cup flour
3 tablespoons butter, melted
½ cup chopped pecans

Directions

For the crust: Mix flour, salt, and sugar. Cut in shortening with fingers or fork until mixture resembles small peas. Add just enough water to allow entire mixture to stick together. Roll out on floured waxed paper. Press into 9-inch pie plate.

For the filling: Preheat oven to 350°F. Put pumpkin in large mixing bowl. Blend with spices. Mix by hand until completely blended. Add eggs, sugars, molasses, butter, and evaporated milk. Mix until smooth. Pour into prepared pie shell.

For the topping: Put brown sugar and flour in bowl and mix. Add chopped pecans and melted butter. Spread over pumpkin pie.

Bake for 50 to 60 minutes or until topping is golden brown. Serve warm or chilled.

Californese Raisin and Nut Pie

John Michael Lerma, St. Paul, MN 2011 APC Crisco National Pie Championships Professional Division Honorable Mention California Raisin

Ingredients

CRUST

1 ½ cups all-purpose flour

½ tablespoon white granulated sugar

½ teaspoon sea salt

¼ cup Crisco butter-flavored shortening, chilled and cut into small pieces

¼ cup cold unsalted butter, cut into small pieces

¼ cup cold water

1 egg yolk and 1 teaspoon water for egg wash

Cooking spray

FILLING

3 large eggs, beaten

$^1/_3$ cup unsalted butter, melted

1 cup white granulated sugar

1 teaspoon pure vanilla extract or vanilla bean paste

1 tablespoon distilled white vinegar

$^1/_3$ cup chopped pecans

$^1/_3$ cup shredded coconut

1 cup raisins

Directions

For the crust: All ingredients should be cold. Combine all the dry ingredients in a large mixing bowl. Add shortening and butter. Using a pastry blender, cut in the shortening and butter until the mixture resembles coarse meal. Drop by drop, add the cold water. Mix in with the fingertips, not hands, as the palms will warm the dough. Continue mixing water in until the dough begins to hold together without being sticky but not crumbly.

Place dough in plastic wrap. Fold over plastic wrap and press down to form a disc. This will make rolling out easier after chilling. Finish wrapping in plastic and place in the refrigerator for at least a half hour. Lightly spray a 9-inch pie plate with cooking spray. Roll out dough and place in pie plate. Remove excess dough and crimp. Brush bottom and sides of crust with egg wash. Return to the refrigerator until filling is ready. Makes pastry for one 9-inch single-crust pie.

For the filling: Preheat oven to 350°F. In a medium mixing bowl, combine eggs, butter, sugar, vanilla extract, and vinegar. Beat until smooth. Stir in pecans, coconut, and raisins. Pour mixture into pastry shell. Bake for 40 minutes. Cool before serving.

Raisin

"Lovin' Spoonful" Cinnamon Roll Raisin Custard Pie

Karen Hall, Elm Creek, NE 2011 APC Crisco National Pie Championships Amateur Division 2nd Place California Raisin

Ingredients

CRUST

3 cups unbleached flour

1 cup plus 1 tablespoon butter-flavored Crisco, cold

½ teaspoon baking powder

1 egg

1 teaspoon sea salt

¼ cup plus 1 tablespoon ice-cold water

1 tablespoon sugar

1 tablespoon rice vinegar

CINNAMON ROLLS

1 container crescent rolls, butter-flavor or original

1 tablespoon butter, melted

2 teaspoons cinnamon sugar

RAISIN CUSTARD FILLING

1 cup California raisins

2½ cups whole milk

3 eggs, beaten

¾ cup sugar

1 tablespoon flour

¼ teaspoon cinnamon

2 teaspoons vanilla extract

2 to 3 drops yellow food color, optional

CINNAMON ROLL ICING

2 oz. cream cheese, softened

1 cup powdered sugar

1 tablespoon milk

1 tablespoon butter, softened

Directions

For the crust: In a large bowl, combine flour, baking powder, salt, and sugar. With a pastry blender, cut in Crisco until mixture resembles coarse crumbs. In a small bowl, beat egg, water, and vinegar together. Add egg mixture slowly while tossing with fork until mixture is moistened (do not overmix). Divide dough and shape into 3 balls. Flatten each to form disc. Wrap each disc with plastic wrap and refrigerate at least 30 minutes before using. Makes three 9-inch, single crusts. Use one disc for this recipe.

For the cinnamon rolls: Preheat oven to 375°F. Unroll crescent rolls from container. Leave in a rectangle shape. Brush top side with butter; sprinkle with cinnamon sugar. Roll into a log lengthwise; pinch seams. Cut log into 20 miniature cinnamon rolls. Place on ungreased cookie sheet. Bake for 8 to 10 minutes or until golden. Set aside.

For the filling: Preheat oven to 425°F. Prepare and roll out pastry for one 9-inch single-crust pie. Line pie dish with pastry. Crimp edge. Arrange raisins into bottom of pie shell. In a medium saucepan, heat milk over medium heat until hot (do not boil), whisking constantly. Remove from heat. In a medium mixing bowl, combine beaten eggs, sugar, flour, cinnamon, vanilla, and yellow food color (optional). Mix until ingredients are well blended. Slowly pour and whisk mixture into hot milk. Blend well. Carefully pour custard into pie shell. Place miniature cinnamon rolls onto custard filling, distributing evenly. Bake at 425°F for 8 minutes. Reduce oven to 350°F. Protect edge of pie with foil to prevent overbrowning. Bake at 350°F for 30 to 35 minutes, or until center is set. Chill pie.

For the cinnamon roll icing: In a small bowl, combine softened cream cheese, powdered sugar, milk, and butter. Stir until smooth. Before serving, pipe icing in a swirling pattern onto each cinnamon roll on top of chilled pie.

California Sunshine Raisin Pie

Patricia Lapiezo, LaMesa, CA 2011 APC Crisco National Pie Championships Amateur Division 1st Place California Raisin

Ingredients

CRUST

3 cups all-purpose flour

1 teaspoon salt

1 cup plus 2 tablespoons Crisco shortening

1 egg, lightly beaten

5 tablespoons ice water

1 tablespoon vinegar

FILLING

2 cups seedless golden raisins

½ cup boiling water

¼ teaspoon salt

2 tablespoons cornstarch

⅓ cup fresh orange juice

2 teaspoons grated orange rind

1 teaspoon grated lemon rind

2 tablespoons butter

TOPPING

(2) 8 oz. packages cream cheese, softened

½ cup granulated sugar

1 teaspoon vanilla

¼ cup sour cream

2 large eggs

¼ cup whipping cream

1 teaspoon lemon juice

½ teaspoon grated lemon rind

¼ teaspoon cinnamon

Directions

For the crust: Preheat oven to 400°F. Combine flour and salt in medium bowl. Cut in shortening. Mix the water, egg, and vinegar. Gradually stir into flour until moistened and dough comes together. Divide in half and form into two discs. Chill at least 30 minutes. On a floured surface, roll out one disc to fit a 10-inch-deep pie pan. Place in pan and flute edges. Prick bottom and sides with a fork and place pie weights in pie pan. Bake blind for 15 minutes. Remove weights and bake an additional 10 minutes or until crust is light golden brown. Cool while preparing filling. Decrease oven temperature to 350°F.

For the filling: Place raisins in a medium saucepan with water, sugar, and salt. Heat to boiling. Mix cornstarch and orange juice. Stir into raisin mixture and cook over low heat, stirring constantly until thick. Remove from heat, then add orange and lemon rind and butter. Stir well and set aside.

For the topping: In a large mixing bowl, beat cream cheese until light and fluffy. Beat in sugar until well blended. Blend in vanilla and sour cream. Add eggs, one at a time, beating lightly after each addition. Stir in whipping cream. Measure out 2 tablespoons butter in a small cup and stir in cinnamon until well blended. Place this in a small pastry bag with a small writing tip.

Spread raisin mixture into bottom of pie crust. Pour cheese topping over raisins. With the pastry bag filling, pipe graduating concentric circles from center to within 1-inch of edge of crust. With a sharp knife or toothpick, draw 8 lines from center to edge of crust, alternating directions. Bake for 35 to 40 minutes or until topping is set and edges are light golden brown. Remove and cool for a half hour. Refrigerate at least 2 hours.

California Raisin Maple Crunch Pie

Patricia Lapiezo, La Mesa, CA 2009 APC Crisco National Pie Championships Amateur Division 1ˢᵗ Place California Raisin

Ingredients

CRUST

1¼ cups all-purpose flour

¼ cup powdered sugar

¼ cup plus 2 tablespoons finely chopped pecans

¹/₈ teaspoon salt

½ cup Crisco butter-flavored shortening

3 tablespoons ice water

FILLING

½ cup butter, melted

½ cup light brown sugar, packed

½ cup light corn syrup

¼ cup maple syrup

¹/₈ teaspoon salt

½ teaspoon vanilla flavoring

3 large eggs, lightly beaten

4 crunchy granola bars, crushed (yields about ¾ cup)

½ cup chopped pecans

¼ cup mini maple or butterscotch chips

1 cup California raisins

Directions

For the crust: Combine flour, powdered sugar, finely chopped pecans, and salt. Cut in shortening until flour is blended to form pea-size chunks. Sprinkle mixture with water, 1 tablespoon at a time. Toss lightly with fork until dough forms a ball. Form a disc. Roll and press crust into a 9-inch pie plate. Set aside while preparing filling.

For the filling: Preheat oven to 350°F. In a large bowl, combine the butter, brown sugar, corn syrup, and maple syrup until blended. Beat in salt, vanilla flavoring, and eggs. Stir in crushed granola bars, pecans, maple chips, and raisins. Bake 40 to 50 minutes, or until filling is set and crust is golden. Cool, then refrigerate. Decorate with sweetened whipped cream, if desired.

Chocolate Raisin Walnut Pie

Andrea Spring, Bradenton, FL 2010 APC Crisco National Pie Championships Professional Division 1st Place and Best of Show California Raisin

Ingredients

CRUST

1½ cups Crisco shortening

1 teaspoon white vinegar

2 tablespoons milk

½ cup hot water

4 cups all-purpose flour

2 teaspoons salt

1 tablespoon cornstarch

FILLING

3 eggs

⅔ cup granulated white sugar

¼ teaspoon cinnamon

1 teaspoon vanilla extract

⅓ cup butter, melted

1 cup dark corn syrup

¾ cup milk chocolate chips

1 cup dark raisins

¾ cup chopped walnuts

Directions

For the crust: Combine shortening, vinegar, and milk. Pour in hot water. Mix well. In separate bowl, mix together flour, salt, and cornstarch. Combine flour mixture with shortening mixture until dough forms. Separate into four equal balls. Wrap in plastic wrap and refrigerate 1 portion for at least one hour before rolling out. Freeze remainder for future use. Roll out one portion of pie dough. Place in 10-inch pie pan.

For the filling: Preheat oven to 400°F. Sprinkle raisins over bottom of pie shell. Mix eggs, vanilla extract, sugar, cinnamon, butter, and corn syrup until well blended. Add chocolate chips and walnuts. Mix well. Set aside. Carefully pour filling over raisins. Bake for 10 minutes at 400°F. Lower temperature to 350°F and bake for 30 minutes or until center of pie is just set. Garnish with whipped cream and chocolate-covered raisins if desired.

Helen's Apple Cider Raisin Pie

Bryan Ehrenholm, Modesto, CA 2010 APC Crisco National Pie Championships Professional Division Honorable Mention California Raisin

Ingredients

CRUST

2 cups all-purpose flour

1 teaspoon salt

1 cup Crisco shortening, chilled

½ cup ice water

FILLING

1 cup raisins

2 cups apple cider (store bottled is fine)

1 cup canned milk

1 cup sugar

1 tablespoon flour

½ teaspoon cinnamon

¼ teaspoon nutmeg

¼ teaspoon cloves

2 eggs, beaten

Directions

For the crust: Place dry ingredients in a mixing bowl and mix together (you can use an electric mixer). Slowly add in chilled shortening and mix until mixture resembles coarse crumbs. Slowly add in ice water until dough forms (you may not use all the water). Place dough on floured surface and roll out into crust about 1/16 inch in thickness. Do not overwork dough. Dough may be refrigerated overnight. You may prepare crust, place in pie dish, and freeze until ready to use. Recipe makes enough dough for 2 single-use crusts or 1 double-crust pie. Preheat oven to 400°F.

Lightly poke the dough with the tip of a fork all over to prevent pie crust from bubbling up. Place tin foil or parchment paper over crust and fill with dried beans or pie weights and bake for 15 to 20 minutes until crust is set. Remove the foil/parchment paper with beans and bake crust for another 15 minutes, until crust is lightly browned. Remove from oven and let cool.

For the filling: Place raisins and apple cider in saucepan and bring to a boil. Gently boil until raisins plump up and are tender. Drain raisins in colander, return them to pan, add canned milk, sugar, flour, and spices. Cook 5 minutes until mixture starts to boil. Add beaten eggs and continually stir until mixture thickens. Pour into pre-baked pie crust. Cool completely and top with your favorite whipped topping. Garnish the top with a sprinkle of cinnamon or raisins.

Californese Raisin and Nut Pie

John Michael Lerma, St. Paul, MN 2011 APC Crisco National Pie Championships Professional Division Honorable Mention California Raisin

Ingredients

CRUST

1½ cups all-purpose flour

½ tablespoon white granulated sugar

½ teaspoon sea salt

¼ cup Crisco butter-flavored shortening, chilled and cut into small pieces

¼ cup cold unsalted butter, cut into small pieces

¼ cup cold water

1 egg yolk and 1 teaspoon water for egg wash

Cooking spray

FILLING

3 large eggs, beaten

$1/3$ cup unsalted butter, melted

1 cup white granulated sugar

1 teaspoon pure vanilla extract or vanilla bean paste

1 tablespoon distilled white vinegar

$1/3$ cup chopped pecans

$1/3$ cup shredded coconut

1 cup raisins

Directions

For the crust: All ingredients should be cold. Combine all the dry ingredients in a large mixing bowl. Add shortening and butter. Using a pastry blender, cut in the shortening and butter until the mixture resembles coarse meal. Drop by drop, add the cold water. Mix in with the fingertips, not hands, as the palms will warm the dough. Continue adding water until the dough begins to hold together but isn't sticky.

Place dough in plastic wrap. Fold over plastic wrap and press down to form a disc. This will make rolling out easier after chilling. Finish wrapping in plastic and place in the refrigerator for at least a half hour. Lightly spray a 9-inch pie plate with cooking spray. Roll out dough and place in pie plate. Remove excess dough and crimp. Brush bottom and sides of crust with egg wash. Return to the refrigerator until filling is ready. Makes pastry for one 9-inch single-crust pie.

For the filling: Preheat oven to 350°F. In a medium mixing bowl, combine eggs, butter, sugar, vanilla extract, and vinegar. Beat until smooth. Stir in pecans, coconut, and raisins. Pour mixture into pastry shell. Bake for 40 minutes. Cool before serving.

Raspberry

Double Chocolate Raspberry Dream Pie

Alberta Dunbar, San Diego, CA 2011 APC Crisco National Pie Championships Amateur Division 1st Place Crisco Classic Chocolate

Ingredients

CRUST
1 1/3 cups all-purpose flour
½ teaspoon salt
½ stick Crisco all-vegetable shortening
3 to 6 tablespoons ice water

FILLING 1
8 oz. cream cheese, softened
1 teaspoon raspberry extract
12 oz. semi-sweet chocolate, melted and cooled
¾ cup heavy cream, whipped

FILLING 2
8 oz. cream cheese, softened
1 teaspoon raspberry extract
12 oz. milk chocolate, melted and cooled
¾ cup heavy cream, whipped

TOPPING
2 cups fresh raspberries
1 cup raspberry jam, melted and cooled
2 cups heavy whipping cream
¼ cup powdered sugar, sifted
1 teaspoon rum extract

Directions

For the crust: Preheat oven to 400°F. Spoon flour into measuring cup and level. Mix flour and salt in a medium bowl. Cut in shortening using pastry blender or 2 knives until flour is blended and forms pea-size chunks. Sprinkle with water 1 tablespoon at a time. Toss lightly with a fork until dough forms a ball. Roll on lightly floured board to fit a 9-inch pie plate with a half-inch overlap. Turn into pie plate, flute edges, and prick bottom with fork. Bake for 10 minutes or until golden brown. Cool on rack completely before filling.

For filling 1: Place cream cheese and extract in a medium bowl and beat on high with electric mixer until smooth. Beat in cooled chocolate. Use wooden spoon to fold in whipped cream. Carefully spread in cooled pie shell. Smooth top and chill for 30 minutes.

For filling 2: Repeat instructions for first filling, using milk chocolate instead of semi-sweet chocolate.

For the topping: In small bowl, combine raspberries and jam. Spread evenly over second layer. Chill for 30 minutes. In medium bowl, combine whipped cream, powdered sugar, and rum extract; beat on high speed until stiff. Fill pastry bag with whipped cream. Fit bag with large rosette tip and pipe large swirls around outer edge of pie. Chill until ready to serve.

Dark Chocolate Raspberry Glacier Pie

Stan C. Strom, Gilbert, AZ 2010 APC Crisco National Pie Championships Amateur Division 1st Place Crisco Classic Chocolate

Ingredients

CRUST

2 cups all-purpose flour (slightly tossed with fork in bag, gently scooped and leveled, but not sifted)

1 cup Soft As Silk cake flour

½ teaspoon kosher salt

½ cup Crisco butter-flavored vegetable shortening, chilled

½ cup butter or lard, chilled

3 tablespoons sugar

1 tablespoon cider vinegar

1 large egg, beaten

1/3 cup ice water

CHOCOLATE RASPBERRY CUSTARD LAYER

1 egg white, lightly beaten, plus 4 large eggs

1 cup International Delight chocolate raspberry coffee creamer (or substitute French vanilla creamer)

2 cups heavy cream

¾ cup sugar

¼ teaspoon salt

1½ teaspoon pure Watkins vanilla extract

1 teaspoon Watkins raspberry extract

12 oz. Hershey's special dark chocolate chips, melted

DARK CHOCOLATE GANACHE

1 cup heavy cream

6 oz. (½ bag) Hershey's semi-sweet or special dark chocolate chips

RASPBERRY TOPPING & GLAZE

2 to 3 pints fresh raspberries

¼ cup raspberry seedless jam

1 tablespoon water

Directions

For the crust: After measuring, sift flour, sugar, and salt. Cut in shortening and butter with a pastry blender until coarse in texture (pea-sized bits). Mix vinegar, beaten egg, and ice water in a small bowl, then add liquid to flour mix until just dampened, mixing with fork. Divide. Place on wide plastic wrap and gather into ball from the outside corners. Chill for at least 30 minutes. Roll out between two layers of wide plastic wrap and fit into 9-inch (deep-dish) glass pie pan. Flute with fork or fingers. Chill for 30 minutes or freeze 15 minutes. Preheat oven to 350°F. This recipe will make enough for one large, 9-inch deep-dish pie with cutouts, or one 9-inch double-crust pie. Bake for 20 to 22 minutes until slightly browned.

For the custard filling: In a heavy saucepan, combine the creamer and cream, and heat until mixture just comes to a simmer. Whisk the 4 large eggs, ¾ cup sugar, salt, and vanilla together to combine. Add the hot milk mixture to the egg-sugar mixture and whisk to blend.

Transfer custard mixture to the blind-baked pie shell and bake at 350°F until the custard is set but still slightly wobbly in the center, 40 to 45 minutes. Transfer to a wire rack to cool. When cooled, transfer to the refrigerator to chill.

For the chocolate ganache: Heat cream in a saucepan over medium heat until hot, but not boiling. Remove pan from heat and stir in chocolate chips. Let rest for 7 to 10 minutes and then stir until smooth. Allow ganache to cool to room temperature, then stir again until smooth and pour over cooled custard.

For the raspberry topping and glaze: In a small saucepan, simmer the jam and water for five minutes, but do not boil. Remove from heat and cool. Brush raspberries with glaze and arrange berries upright on top of ganache. Refrigerate overnight.

Chocolate Raspberry Delight Pie

Michelle Stuart, Norwalk, CT 2011 APC National Pie Championships Professional Division Honorable Mention Crisco Classic Chocolate

Ingredients

CRUST

2 cups flour

1 teaspoon salt

¾ cup Crisco

5 tablespoons very cold water

Cream to brush on pie crust edge

RASPBERRY GLACÉ

1 cup fresh raspberries, mashed

1 cup sugar

3 tablespoons cornstarch

½ cup water

FILLING 1

¾ cup plus 2 tablespoons sugar

3½ tablespoons cornstarch

$^1/_8$ teaspoon salt

2½ cups whole milk

4 large egg yolks

2 tablespoons unsalted butter

2 teaspoons vanilla

3 oz. unsweetened chocolate, chopped

$^1/_8$ cup semi-sweet chocolate chips

½ cup raspberry glace (recipe below)

½ cup brownie chunks (recipe below)

Chocolate whipped cream (recipe below)

Raspberries for garnish

BROWNIE CHUNKS

4 oz. unsweetened chocolate

¾ cup butter

1$^1/_3$ cups flour

½ teaspoon salt

1 teaspoon baking powder

4 eggs

2 cups sugar

2 teaspoons vanilla

1 cup chocolate chips

CHOCOLATE WHIPPED CREAM

2 cups heavy cream

1 teaspoon vanilla

Confectionary sugar to taste

¼ cup cooled hot fudge sauce (recipe below)

HOT FUDGE SAUCE

1 cup sugar

3 cups heavy cream

¼ cup light corn syrup

4 oz. unsweetened chocolate

¼ cup butter

1 tablespoon vanilla extract

Directions

For the crust: Combine flour and salt in a mixing bowl. Cut Crisco into the flour mixture until coarse crumbs form. Add water 1 tablespoon at a time, mixing gently until incorporated and dough can form a ball. Wrap dough in plastic and refrigerate for at least 30 minutes. Preheat oven to 425°F. Divide dough in half. Use only half the dough for this recipe. Roll out and place pastry in a 9-inch pan. Brush the edge of pie crust with cream. Bake for 15 to 20 minutes or until golden brown. Let the crust cool completely before filling.

For the raspberry glacé: Combine the mashed raspberries, sugar, cornstarch, and water in a medium-sized saucepan over high heat. Stir while the ingredients cook, for about 10 minutes or until the mixture attains a thick consistency. Be patient, this does take time, but it is worth it! Let the glacé cool to room temperature and then place in the refrigerator prior to use.

For the brownie chunks: preheat oven to 350°F. Grease a half sheet pan. Melt chocolate and butter in saucepan over low heat, stirring constantly until smooth. Remove from heat and set aside. Mix flour, salt, and baking powder in a separate bowl. In another bowl, beat eggs thoroughly. Gradually beat sugar into eggs until thoroughly combined. Add the flour mixture to the egg mixture and combine well. Blend in chocolate mixture and vanilla. Stir well. Add chocolate chips, mixing well. Bake for 25 minutes. Cool in pan. Cut into chunks.

For the filling: Combine the sugar, cornstarch, and salt in a saucepan. Whisk to mix thoroughly. Whisk in egg yolks and milk. Place over medium heat and cook. Whisk nonstop until mixture starts to bubble and thicken. Once it thickens, add butter one tablespoon at a time. Then add the vanilla. Once all mixed together, add the chocolate, ⅓ of the amount at a time. Remove from heat once all the chocolate is melted and mixture has thickened. Allow the cream to cool in a bowl in the refrigerator for about 15 minutes. Add the chocolate chips and brownie chunks, mixing until combined.

Spread raspberry glacé evenly on the bottom of the pie shell. Pour chocolate mixture in pie shell over the raspberry glacé. Cover with wrap and refrigerate for at least 3 hours.

Once chilled, remove plastic wrap from pie.

For the whipped cream: Mix together cream, vanilla, and sugar with an electric mixer on high speed until creamy.

For the hot fudge sauce: Combine all the ingredients, except the vanilla, in a medium saucepan. Bring the mixture to a boil over medium-high heat. Whisk constantly for 5 minutes over heat. Once it looks like the sauce is separating, remove from heat and add vanilla. Chill sauce until it thickens, about 5 hours.

Add hot fudge sauce to whipped cream mixture and beat until stiff peaks form.

Top pie with chocolate whipped cream and raspberries for garnish. Serve cold.

Key Lime–Raspberry Pie

George Yates, Dallas, TX 2011 APC Crisco National Pie Championships Amateur Division 1st Place Citrus

Ingredients

CRUST

1½ cups crushed gingersnap crumbs

½ cup crushed vanilla wafer crumbs

¼ cup toasted almonds, ground

3 tablespoons sugar

5 tablespoons unsalted butter, melted

1 teaspoon key lime juice

KEY LIME CURD

3 eggs plus 4 egg yolks

1 cup sugar

1 tablespoon grated lime zest

½ cup fresh key lime juice

4 tablespoons unsalted butter, softened

1/8 teaspoon salt

KEY LIME FILLING

1 tablespoon unflavored gelatin

2/3 cup water

1 cup sugar, divided

2/3 cup fresh key lime juice

5 eggs, separated

1 tablespoon freshly grated key lime zest

4 oz. white chocolate, melted

RASPBERRY FILLING

1 cup fresh raspberries

1 cup water, divided

1 cup sugar

3 tablespoons cornstarch

3 tablespoons raspberry gelatin

2 tablespoons seedless raspberry jam

2 teaspoons key lime zest

GARNISH

2 cups whipping cream

4 tablespoons confectioner's sugar, raspberries, sliced limes, sliced almonds, raspberry jam

Directions

For the crust: Preheat oven to 350°F. In a medium bowl, combine crumbs, ground almonds, and sugar. Stir key lime juice into melted butter until combined. Add butter mixture to crumb mixture until well-blended. Press crumb mixture into 10-inch deep-dish pie pan with 2-inch sides and bake for 10 minutes. Cool completely before filling.

For the curd: Whisk eggs, yolks, and sugar in a saucepan until thick. Whisk in zest, juice, butter, and salt. Cook over medium-low heat, stirring constantly until very smooth and thick. Remove from heat. Cool to room temperature. Refrigerate.

For the key lime filling: In a heavy-bottomed saucepan, sprinkle the gelatin over the water and let stand for a few minutes to soften. Add ½ cup sugar and the key lime juice. Mix well. Then add the egg yolks and whisk until blended. Place over moderate heat and cook, stirring constantly, until the mixture thickens slightly and barely reaches a simmer, 5 to 10 minutes; do not allow it to boil. Stir in the key lime zest and the melted white chocolate. Pour the gelatin mixture into a bowl and refrigerate, stirring occasionally, for about 1 hour.

In a medium bowl, beat the 5 egg whites until soft peaks form, then gradually add the remaining ⅓ cup sugar and beat until stiff peaks form. Gently fold the key lime mixture into the whites and pour half the filling into pie crust. Chill until firm. Mix raspberry filling (follows) and assemble.

For the raspberry filling: Place raspberries and ⅔ cup water in a saucepan. Simmer for 3 minutes. Whisk sugar, cornstarch, and remaining ⅓ cup water in a small bowl until smooth; add to raspberry mixture. Boil one minute, whisking constantly. Remove from heat. Add gelatin, whisking until smooth. Stir in jam until smooth. Strain through a sieve to remove seeds and stir in key lime zest. Cool to room temperature. Spread the rasberry filling over the chilled key lime filling layer in pie crust. Spread the remaining key lime filling over raspberry filling. Chill until firm.

Spread curd over filling. Chill again for several hours or overnight.

For the garnish: Beat together whipping cream and confectioner's sugar. Garnish pie with whipped cream, raspberries, sliced limes, and sliced almonds. Drizzle with raspberry jam.

Raspberry Lemonade Pie

Patricia Lapiezo, LaMesa, CA 2006 APC Crisco National Pie Championships Amateur Division 1st Place Citrus

Ingredients

CRUST
3 cups all-purpose flour
1¼ cups Crisco shortening
1 teaspoon salt
5 tablespoons ice water
1 tablespoon vinegar
1 egg, slightly beaten

1 tablespoon granulated sugar
½ cup fresh raspberries
12 oz. cream cheese, softened
6 oz. can frozen raspberry lemonade
   concentrate, thawed
14 oz. can sweetened condensed milk
1½ cups heavy cream, stiffly beaten

FILLING
10 oz. box frozen sweetened
   raspberries, thawed
1 tablespoon cornstarch

GARNISH
Sweetened whipped cream
Lemon slice
Raspberries

Directions

For the crust: Preheat oven to 400°F. Combine flour and salt in large bowl. Cut in shortening. In a small bowl, combine egg, water, and vinegar. Gradually add liquid to flour mixture until dough comes together. Refrigerate 1 hour. Roll out one half of dough to fit a 10-inch-deep pie pan. Prebake crust for 12–15 minutes or until golden brown. Cool.

For the filling: Puree the thawed raspberries until smooth. Strain. Place puree, cornstarch, and sugar in a small saucepan and stir until combined. Cook over medium heat until mixture thickens. Reserve ¼ cup and pour remaining mixture in bottom of crust.

In a large mixing bowl, beat the cream cheese until softened. Beat in sweetened condensed milk until well blended. Add raspberry lemonade, reserved ¼ cup raspberry puree, and ½ cup fresh raspberries, beating until blended. Fold in whipped cream. Pour over first layer, smoothing top.

Decorate with sweetened whipped cream, a lemon slice, and raspberries, if desired. Refrigerate 1 hour.

Lemon Raspberry Twist

Michele Stuart, Norwalk, CT 2011 APC Crisco National Pie Champion-ships Professional Division 1ˢᵗ Place Citrus

Ingredients

CRUST

2 cups flour

1 teaspoon salt

¾ cup Crisco

5 tablespoons very cold water

Cream to brush on pie crust edge

Raspberry Glace

1 cup fresh raspberries, mashed

1 cup sugar

3 tablespoons cornstarch

½ cup water

LEMON CHIFFON FILLING

1 whole egg

2 egg yolks

½ cup sugar

¼ cup cornstarch

Pinch of salt

1 cup lemon juice

1 cup hot water

2 tablespoons unsalted butter

1 tablespoon lemon zest

1 teaspoon water, room temperature
    (for the gelatin)

1 teaspoon gelatin

MERINGUE

4 large egg whites, room
    temperature

¼ teaspoon cream of tartar

Pinch of salt

½ cup sugar

1 teaspoon vanilla

GARNISH

Whipped cream

Lemon zest

Raspberries

Directions

For the crust: Preheat oven to 425°F. Combine flour and salt in a mixing bowl. Cut Crisco into the flour mixture until coarse crumbs form. Add water 1 tablespoon at a time, mixing gently until incorporated and dough can form a ball. Wrap dough in plastic and refrigerate for at least 30 minutes. Divide dough in half. Use only half the dough for this recipe. Roll out and place pastry in a 9-inch pan. Brush the edge of pie crust with cream. Bake for 15 to 20 minutes or until golden brown. Let the crust cool completely before filling.

For the raspberry glacé: Combine the mashed raspberries, sugar, cornstarch, and water in a medium-sized saucepan over high heat. Stir while the ingredients cook, for about 10 minutes or until the mixture attains a thick consistency. Be patient, this does take time, but it is worth it! Let the glace cool to room temperature and then place in the refrigerator prior to use. Spread 1 cup raspberry glace on bottom of prepared pie shell.

For the lemon chiffon filling: In a small bowl, add the teaspoon of water to the gelatin. Set aside so gelatin can soften while filling is prepared.

Whisk the egg, egg yolks, and sugar together in a medium bowl. Still whisking, add the cornstarch and salt. Mix in the lemon juice, hot water, butter, and lemon zest.

Transfer the filling to a medium saucepan and cook over medium heat, scraping the sides of the pan frequently to prevent any burning. Whisk continuously until the mixture becomes bubbly and thick, for about 5 minutes. Add the gelatin to the filling, folding it in until all ingredients are combined.

For the meringue: In a separate mixing bowl, beat the egg whites until foamy. Add cream of tartar and salt. Beat until soft peaks form. Then add the sugar 1 tablespoon at a time. After all the sugar has been added, mix in the vanilla, beating for about 30 seconds. Once complete, gently fold the meringue into the lemon filling so that they are thoroughly combined. Place the lemon filling over the raspberry glacé. Chill pie overnight.

Garnish with whipped cream, lemon zest, and raspberries.

Raspberry Smoothie Cream Pie

Carol Socier, Bay City, MI 2010 APC Crisco National Pie Championships Amateur Division 1st Place Cream

Ingredients

CRUST

1½ cups all-purpose flour
1 tablespoon sugar
¼ teaspoon salt
½ cup Crisco shortening
¼ cup toasted almonds, finely crushed
¼ cup white chocolate chips
3 to 4 tablespoons ice cold water
2 teaspoons light cream

FILLING

4.6 oz. package Jell-O Cook & Serve
vanilla pudding mix
1½ cups half and half
8 oz. raspberry cream cheese spread
10 oz. carton frozen raspberries in
syrup
1 tablespoon cornstarch
3 cups fresh raspberries, divided
1 cup whipping cream, whipped and
sweetened

Directions

For the crust: Preheat oven to 450°F. Combine flour, sugar, and salt. Cut in shortening until pea-sized pieces form. Stir in crushed almonds. Sprinkle in water, l tablespoon at a time, gently tossing with a fork until mixture is moistened and forms a ball. On lightly floured surface, roll out dough into a 12-inch circle; transfer to a 9-inch pie plate. Trim half-inch inch from the edge. Fold under the extra pastry and flute the edge. Prick bottom and sides of the crust. Bake 12 to 15 minutes or until golden brown. Cool. Melt chips and cream; brush bottom and sides of cooled crust.

For the filling: Cook the pudding mix according to package directions, but use 1½ cups half and half for the liquid. Cool for 20 minutes. Beat in the cream cheese spread. Spread into bottom of prepared pie crust. Chill for 1 hour.

Meanwhile, prepare the glaze. Puree the frozen raspberries. In a small saucepan, combine berries and cornstarch. Cook and stir over medium heat until thick and bubbly. Cool to room temperature. Assemble the pie by placing half the fresh raspberries, stem side down, over the cream layer. Drizzle glaze over the berries. Garnish with whipped cream and remaining raspberries.

Royal Macadamia Raspberry Pie

Phyllis Szymanek, Toledo, OH 2011 APC Crisco National Pie Championships 1st Place Cream Cheese and Best of Show

Ingredients

CRUST
1½ cups Pillsbury all-purpose flour
½ cup Crisco
½ teaspoon salt
3 tablespoons butter (chilled)
3 to 4 tablespoons ice water
2 tablespoons chopped macadamia
   nuts

GLAZE
1 cup sugar
2½ tablespoons corn starch

1¼ cups water
Pinch of salt
3 oz. box raspberry Jell-O
3 cups raspberries

CREAM CHEESE FILLING
8 oz. package cream cheese
   (softened)
½ cup powdered sugar
½ teaspoon lemon juice
8 oz. Cool Whip
½ cup chopped macadamia nuts

Directions

For the crust: Preheat oven to 425°F. In a mixing bowl, combine flour and salt; cut in Crisco and butter until crumbly. Add water one tablespoon at a time until dough forms into a ball. Chill for one hour. Roll out on floured surface to fit a 9-inch pie dish. Lightly press macadamia nuts into pie crust. Place in pie dish and bake for 12 to 15 minutes or until lightly brown. Set aside to cool.

For the glaze: In a small saucepan, combine sugar, cornstarch, water, and salt over medium heat. Bring to a boil. Boil until thick and clear. Remove from heat and add Jell-O. Mix well. Set aside and cool for 15 to 20 minutes

For the cream cheese filling: Place cream cheese in a medium mixing bowl and beat on low speed until creamy. Add powdered sugar until mixed well. Add lemon juice. Fold in ½ of the Cool Whip. Spread ½ of the cream cheese mixture onto bottom cooled pie crust. Spread ½ of raspberries over cream cheese. Pour

½ glaze over raspberries. Refrigerate for 15 to 20 minutes. Then add remaining cream cheese over raspberries; top with remaining raspberries, then the rest of the glaze. Chill for about an hour. Put remaining Cool Whip in a pastry bag with a star tip to garnish top of pie, making three circles around outer edge of pie. Sprinkle with nuts.

Linda's Luscious Raspberry Custard

Phyllis Bartholomew, Columbus, NE 2004 APC Crisco National Pie Championships Amateur Division 1st Place Custard

Ingredients

CRUST

2 cups flour

1 cup cake flour

1 cup Crisco shortening, butter-flavored

1 whole egg

1 tablespoon cider vinegar

½ teaspoon salt

⅓ cup ice water

FILLING

3 eggs

14 oz. can Eagle brand sweetened condensed milk

1 ¼ cups hot water

1 teaspoon pure vanilla extract

¼ teaspoon salt

⅛ teaspoon cinnamon

2 cups fresh or frozen raspberries

Directions

For the crust: Preheat oven to 425°F. Mix the flours and butter powder together. Cut in the shortening until it resembles coarse crumbs. Beat together the other ingredients and stir into the flour. Mix just until incorporated. Form dough into a disc and wrap in plastic wrap. Refrigerate to chill. Roll out about ⅓ of the dough between 2 sheets of plastic wrap. Place crust in a 9-inch pie dish. Bake for about 8 to 10 minutes. Let cool.

For the filling: Preheat oven to 400°F. Beat the eggs in a bowl. Add the water, milk, vanilla, salt, and cinnamon. Mix well. Fold in the raspberries very gently. Pour into the pie shell and arrange the raspberries evenly. Bake for 10 minutes at 400°F on the bottom rack and then reduce heat to 350°F and move the pie to the middle rack. Bake for 25 to 30 minutes more or until knife inserted near the center comes out clean. Cool before serving.

Raspberry Chocolate Mint Ribbon Pie

Beth Campbell, Belleville, WI 2003 APC Crisco National Pie Championships Amateur Division 1st Place Open

Ingredients

CRUST

1 cup flour

½ cup Crisco shortening

¼ cup cold water

Pinch of salt

CHOCOLATE FILLING

1½ sticks butter

1½ cups powdered sugar

5 egg yolks

½ teaspoon peppermint flavoring

3 squares baking chocolate, melted
    and cooled

5 egg whites, stiffly beaten

CREAM CHEESE FILLING

3 oz. cream cheese, softened

$^1/_3$ cup sifted powdered sugar

1 teaspoon vanilla

1 cup heavy whipped cream

RASPBERRY FILLING

(you can substitute 1 cup of seedless
    raspberry jam)

1½ tablespoons sugar

1 cup frozen raspberries

½ tablespoon cornstarch

Directions

For the crust: Preheat oven to 475°F . Cut shortening into salt and flour until pea-sized pieces form. Add cold water slowly until mixture forms a ball. Refrigerate several hours or overnight. Roll out on a floured board. Put in pie pan. Prick crust on bottom of pan with a fork. Bake for 8 to 10 minutes until light brown. Cool.

For the chocolate filling: Cream together butter and powdered sugar. Add egg yolks one yolk at a time. Add peppermint flavoring and melted chocolate. Fold in egg whites.

For the cream cheese filling: Mix together powdered sugar, vanilla, and cream cheese. Fold in whipped cream until smooth.

For the raspberry filling: Cook raspberries in a saucepan over medium-low heat until they are partially cooked. Run raspberries through a cheesecloth or sieve to remove the seeds. Return to heat and add cornstarch. Boil over medium heat. Allow to cool and then spread half of the raspberry filling into baked pie shell gently. Spread half of the chocolate filling over that and chill. Spread half the cream cheese filling over the chocolate filling. Repeat the layers. Refrigerate until ready to serve.

Strawberry

Double Strawberry Malt Shop Pie

Christine Montalvo, Windsor Heights, IA 2011 APC Crisco National Pie Championships 2nd Place Cream Cheese

Ingredients

CRUST

6 tablespoons unsalted butter, at room temperature

¼ cup granulated sugar

1 cup all-purpose flour

1 cup finely ground shortbread cookies

2 to 3 tablespoons ice water

FILLING

5 cups sliced fresh strawberries, divided

6 oz. good quality white chocolate

1¾ teaspoon unflavored gelatin

1 tablespoon hot water

8 oz. package Philadelphia Cream Cheese

1 teaspoon vanilla

1½ cups powdered sugar

1/3 cup malted milk powder

2 cups heavy whipping cream, whipped

TOPPING

1½ cups heavy whipping cream

3 tablespoons sugar

Directions

For the crust: Preheat oven to 350°F. Using an electric mixer, cream the butter and sugar together on medium-high speed until fluffy. Add flour and ground shortbread cookies to the mixture and blend until fully incorporated. Add enough ice water so dough can come together. Press the mixture evenly into the bottom of a 9-inch deep-dish pie plate. Bake the crust for 20 to 25 minutes, or until golden brown. Allow the crust to cool completely.

For the filling: Put 2½ cups of strawberries in a food processor and puree. Set aside. Put all of the chocolate in a large microwave-safe bowl and melt in the microwave, being careful not to burn the chocolate. Cool slightly. Add cream cheese and vanilla, and beat until smooth. In a small bowl, combine gelatin and hot water. Stir and then let sit for 5 minutes. Microwave 15 seconds. Beat into cream cheese mixture until completely mixed. Beat in the powdered sugar and malted milk powder until smooth. Stir in the puree. Fold in the whipped cream. Fold in remaining sliced strawberries. Pour into cooled pie crust. Arrange the additional sliced strawberries over pie.

Whip cream in a large bowl with sugar until stiff peaks form. Pipe decoratively over pie.

My Big Fat Italian Strawberry–Basil Wedding Pie

Naylet LaRochelle, Miami, FL 2011 APC Crisco National Pie Championships Amateur Division 1ˢᵗ Place Crisco Innovation

Ingredients

CRUST

2½ cups flour

1 tablespoon sugar

1 teaspoon salt

½ cup (1 stick) unsalted butter, cold

½ cup Crisco butter-flavored shortening, cold

½ cup finely ground pine nuts

⅓ cup ice water

2 teaspoons white wine vinegar

1 egg

1 tablespoon water

FILLING

1 envelope unflavored gelatin

¼ cup whipping cream, plus ½ cup whipping cream

10 oz. jar Smucker's strawberry spreadable fruit

8 oz. container mascarpone cheese

1 teaspoon pure vanilla extract

Pinch of salt

1 teaspoon grated lemon peel

1½ cups fresh strawberries, crushed

2 tablespoons finely chopped fresh basil leaves

VANILLA BEAN-WHITE CHOCO-LATE MOUSSE TOPPING

¾ cup white chocolate chips

½ cup heavy whipping cream, plus 2 tablespoons

1½ teaspoons vanilla paste

White chocolate curls, for garnish

White fondant flowers, for garnish, if desired

Directions

For the crust: Preheat oven to 425°F. In a large bowl, combine the flour, sugar, and salt. Using a pastry cutter, cut in the butter and shortening. Add the pine nuts. Drizzle the water and vinegar into the flour mixture and combine with hands until a ball of dough is formed. Divide dough in half and shape each half into a flat disc. Refrigerate for about 1 hour to chill dough. On a lightly floured surface, roll out one disc to fit a 9-inch pie plate. Ease pie dough into pie plate; trim pastry edges. Do not prick pastry. Line the pastry with foil; fill with pie weights. Bake 10–12 minutes or until golden brown.

For the filling: In a small microwavable bowl, combine gelatin and ¼ cup whipping cream. Set aside for 5 minutes. Microwave in 30-second intervals, until gelatin is completely dissolved. Let cool 10 minutes. In a large bowl, stir together strawberry spreadable fruit, mascarpone, vanilla extract, salt, lemon peel, and dissolved gelatin mixture until well combined. Add strawberries and basil; stir until combined. In a medium bowl, using an electric mixer, beat on high remaining ½ cup whipping cream until stiff peaks form. Fold into the strawberry mixture. Pour filling into prebaked pie shell. Refrigerate 2 hours, or until filling is set.

For the topping: In a small saucepan, melt white chocolate chips and 2 tablespoons cream, stirring often, over low heat. When chocolate is completely melted, remove from heat. Stir in vanilla paste. Let chocolate cool (but not harden). In a medium bowl, using an electric mixer, beat ½ cup whipping cream until stiff peaks form. Fold whipped cream into cooled white chocolate mixture. Spread over top of pie, or pipe in a decorative manner. Return pie to refrigerator for 2 to 3 hours, or until topping is set. Garnish pie with white chocolate curls.

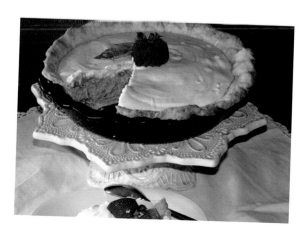

Four Seasons Strawberry–Rhubarb Pie

Evette Rahman, Orlando, FL 2007 APC Crisco National Pie Championships Amateur Division Fruit/Berry

Ingredients

CRUST

2 cups flour

2 tablespoons sugar

¾ teaspoon salt

½ teaspoon baking powder

1/3 cup vegetable shortening

1/3 cup unsalted butter, very cold and cubed

1 tablespoon oil

1 tablespoon vinegar

1/3 cup heavy cream

1 egg white

Sugar for sprinkling

FILLING

16 oz. bag frozen whole strawberries: set out about 45 minutes to thaw slightly

16 oz. bag frozen sliced rhubarb: set out about 45 minutes to thaw slightly (cut into ½ inch pieces and discard any brown or pale-colored pieces)

½ teaspoon orange zest

¼ cup instant tapioca

1 2/3 cups granulated white sugar

2 tablespoons cornstarch

1½ tablespoons salted butter, cubed

Directions

For the crust: Preheat oven to 375°F. Mix together flour, sugar, salt, and baking powder. Cut in shortening and butter. Stir together oil, vinegar, and cream. Add to flour. Form into two discs. Wrap in plastic. Refrigerate for 1 hour. Roll out 1 dough disc on lightly floured cold surface and place in deep-dish pie plate. Blind-bake for 15 minutes. Cool completely. Brush inside with some of the egg white and chill.

For the filling: Preheat oven to 400°F. Combine all filling ingredients, except butter. Cover and set aside for 15 minutes. Fill pie plate and top with butter. Roll out remaining dough into strips and create a lattice-design top crust over filling. (Strips should be made and refrigerated ahead of time.) Cut off excess dough and crimp edges. Mix remaining egg white with 1 teaspoon of water. Brush crust with egg wash and sprinkle with sugar. Put in freezer for 10 minutes. Place in large dark pan and bake at 400°F for 20 minutes, then reduce temperature to 375°F and bake for 1 hour or until bubbly and golden brown. Cover pie edges and top of pie with foil to prevent excess browning. Cool pie completely before cutting.

Glazed Strawberry Cheesecake Pie

Valarie Enters, Sanford, FL 2010 APC Crisco National Pie Championships Professional Division Honorable Mention Fruit/Berry

Ingredients

CRUST

2 cups cinnamon graham crackers,
  crushed

⅓ cup sugar

½ cup butter, melted

FILLING

3 packages cream cheese

½ cup sugar

¼ cup sour cream

1½ teaspoons vanilla

2 eggs

Glaze

1 cup sugar

1 cup water

3 tablespoons Karo syrup

3 tablespoons cornstarch

3 tablespoons gelatin

Pinch salt

Red food color

TOPPING

2 quarts fresh strawberries

Whipped topping and graham cracker
  crumbs for garnish

Directions

For the crust: Preheat oven to 350°F. Mix ingredients together and press into the bottom and sides of a pie pan. Bake for 15 minutes, then let cool.

For the filling: Blend all ingredients together and pour into crust. Bake at 350°F until golden and set, about 30 minutes

For the glaze: Combine all ingredients in a saucepan. Bring to a boil over medium heat, then cool.

For the topping: Hull strawberries and rinse with water. Pat dry and set on paper towels. Dip strawberries in glaze and set on cheesecake. Garnish with whipped topping and graham cracker crumbs.

Fantastico Neapolitan Pie

Alberta Dunbar, San Diego, CA 2011 APC Crisco National Pie Championships Amateur Division 2nd Place No Sugar Added

Ingredients

CRUST

2 cups sugar-free shortbread cookie crumbs

6 tablespoons butter, melted

LAYER 1

4 oz. cream cheese, softened

4 oz. sugar-free dark chocolate, melted and cooled

¾ cup milk

1 oz. package sugar-free vanilla instant pudding

1 teaspoon Kona coffee extract

¾ cup heavy cream, whipped

LAYER 2

4 oz. cream cheese, softened

4 oz. sugar-free white chocolate, melted and cooled

¾ cup milk

1 oz. package sugar-free vanilla instant pudding

1 teaspoon strawberry extract

1 drop red food coloring

¾ cup heavy cream, whipped

1 cup strawberries, diced large

LAYER 3

4 oz. cream cheese, softened

4 oz. sugar-free white chocolate, melted

¾ cup milk

1 oz. package sugar-free instant vanilla pudding

1 teaspoon rum extract

1 drop green food coloring

¾ cup heavy cream, whipped

½ cup ground toasted pistachios (no salt)

TOPPING

2 cups heavy cream

2 tablespoons Splenda

1 teaspoon rum extract

GARNISH

Shredded sugar-free chocolate

Directions

For the crust: Mix ingredients in a small bowl with a fork until well mixed. Press on bottom and sides of 9-inch pie plate. Freeze until ready to use.

For layer 1: Place cream cheese and milk in medium bowl. Beat until well blended and smooth. Beat in cooled chocolate. Add pudding and extract. Beat well with wooden spoon and fold in whipped cream. Carefully spread in pie shell. Smooth top and refrigerate.

For layer 2: Repeat directions for layer 1 with layer 2 ingredients. Carefully fold in strawberries and spread over first layer.

For layer 3: Repeat above instructions for the first two layers with layer 3 ingredients. Fold in pistachios. Spread over second layer. Smooth top and chill until set.

For topping: Place ingredients in medium bowl and beat on high until stiff. Fill pastry bag with medium strips and pipe all over pie. Sprinkle with shredded chocolate if so desired.

Peanut Butter-N-Strawberry Explosion Pie

Erika Werkheiser, Orlando, FL 2008 APC Crisco National Pie Championships Amateur Division 3rd Place Peanut Butter

Ingredients

CRUST
30 vanilla wafers, crushed
¼ tablespoon butter, melted
½ cup strawberry jelly

¾ cup sugar
1¾ cups peanut butter
8 oz. tub frozen whipped topping, thawed

FILLING
8 oz. package (⅓ less fat) cream cheese

GARNISH
Fresh strawberries
Strawberry jelly

Directions

For the crust: Mix vanilla wafers and melted butter together and spread evenly on bottom and sides of pie plate. Chill in refrigerator for 15 to 20 minutes. Spread strawberry jelly evenly on bottom crust. Cover and refrigerate.

For the filling: Beat cream cheese in bowl until smooth. Slowly beat in sugar. Stir in peanut butter and whipped topping until blended. Spoon mixture onto crust over strawberry jelly. Cover. Refrigerate at least 8 hours.

For the garnish: Put fresh strawberries or peanut butter chips on top of pie. Fill a candy decorating bag with strawberry jelly. Decorate pie with the jelly and make swirls in the jelly with a toothpick.

Strawberry Smoothie Splenda Pie

Terri Beaver, Olalla, WA 2009 APC Crisco National Pie Championships Amateur Division 3rd Place Splenda

Ingredients

CRUST (makes two 9-inch pie crusts)
2¾ cups flour, plus extra for rolling
1 teaspoon salt
2 tablespoons Splenda sweetener
10 tablespoons butter-flavored Crisco
6 tablespoons Crisco shortening
½ cup ice water
1 tablespoon apple cider vinegar
1 ice cube

FILLING
16 oz. bag whole frozen strawberries
    (unsweetened), thawed
1 cup Splenda sweetener
½ cup sugar-free strawberry jam
2 envelopes unflavored gelatin

½ cup cold water
4 oz. cream cheese, room
    temperature
½ cup plain yogurt
½ cup heavy cream
1 teaspoon vanilla

GLAZE TOPPING
½ cup Splenda sweetener
1 tablespoon potato starch or
    cornstarch
Reserved strawberry juice
Water
2 drops red food coloring (if desired)
1 pint fresh strawberries, cleaned,
    hulled, and halved

Directions

For the crust: Combine flour, salt, and Splenda in a large bowl. Cut in both shortenings until texture is about the size of small peas. Mix water and vinegar in a small bowl. Add ice cube. (You will not use all of this mixture). One tablespoon at a time, add 6 to 8 tablespoons of water mixture to flour mixture until doughy. Divide into two discs and wrap in plastic wrap. Chill thoroughly, at least 2 hours. You will use one disc for this recipe.

Take one disc and roll out on floured surface. Carefully place in pie plate and flute edges. Put in freezer or refrigerate for at least 30 minutes. Preheat oven to 400°F. Line pie shell with parchment paper and bake with pie weights for 15 minutes. Remove pie weights and lower oven temperature to 375°F. Bake for 12 to 15 minutes. Cover edges with foil or a pie guard if needed. Let cool.

For the filling: Drain strawberries and reserve juice for glaze. Take one half the berries and coarsely chop. Set aside. In a saucepan, sprinkle gelatin over cold water. Let sit for 1 minute. Over medium heat, stir until completely dissolved. Add jam and heat until liquid. Let cool about 10 minutes. Place remaining berries in a blender with the Splenda and puree. Add cream cheese, yogurt, vanilla, and cream. Blend well. Add the jam mixture and blend. Stir in the strawberry pieces. Pour into prepared pie crust. Chill in refrigerator.

For the glaze topping: Mix Splenda and potato starch in a saucepan. Add enough water to the reserved strawberry juice to make 1 cup. Pour into saucepan. Whisk over medium heat until it just comes to a boil. Add red food coloring if desired. Cool to room temperature. Place berries cut side-down on chilled pie. Pour glaze over the top and chill thoroughly before serving.

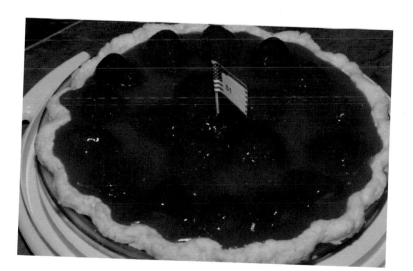

Sweet Potato

Maple Pecan Sweet Potato Pie

Jill Jones, Palm Bay, FL 2011 APC Crisco National Pie Championships Amateur Division 3rd Place Sweet Potato

Ingredients

CRUST

1 cup flour

½ teaspoon salt

¼ tablespoon sugar

½ cup shortening

1 egg

1½ tablespoons ice water

¼ tablespoon vinegar

FILLING

1 cup brown sugar

1 teaspoon cinnamon

2 tablespoons flour

2½ cups mashed sweet potatoes (3 potatoes)

2 eggs, slightly beaten

¼ teaspoon salt

1 teaspoon nutmeg, fresh

5 oz. can evaporated milk

1 teaspoon pure vanilla

¼ teaspoon pumpkin pie spice

1 cup chopped pecans

2 tablespoons maple syrup

Directions

For the crust: Mix flour, sugar, and salt. Cut in shortening with fork or pastry cutter until mix is crumbly. Add egg, vinegar, and water. Mix until it comes together and is slightly sticky. Scrape out of bowl and place on a floured surface. Roll into a ball and wrap in plastic wrap. Refrigerate for 1 hour. Roll out on a floured surface.

For the filling: Preheat oven to 450°F. Mix sugar, cinnamon, flour, salt, nutmeg, and pumpkin pie spice with mashed sweet potatoes. Mix milk, eggs, and vanilla into sweet potato mixture. Pour into unbaked pie shell. Mix pecans and syrup together and spread on top of pie before baking. Bake at 450°F for 15 minutes, then reduce temperature to 325°F for 30 to 45 minutes longer or until done.

Maple Sweet Potato Surprise Pie

Karen Hall, Elm Creek, NE 2007 APC Crisco National Pie Champion-ships Amateur Division 1ˢᵗ Place Sweet Potato

Ingredients

CRUST

3 cups unbleached flour

1 tablespoon buttermilk powder

½ teaspoon baking powder

1 teaspoon salt

1 cup plus 1 tablespoon butter-flavored Crisco cut into ¼-inch parts

1 egg

⅓ cup cold water

1 tablespoon vinegar

CREAM CHEESE LAYER

4 oz. cream cheese, softened

¼ cup sugar

1 egg white

2 tablespoons walnuts, chopped

FILLING

2 cups cooked mashed sweet potato

3 eggs, plus 1 egg yolk, beaten

½ cup light brown sugar, packed

½ cup maple syrup

½ cup evaporated milk

½ teaspoon cinnamon

⅛ teaspoon cloves

⅛ teaspoon ginger

⅛ teaspoon sea salt

CREAM CHEESE ICING

2 oz. cream cheese, softened

½ cup powdered sugar

1 tablespoon milk

GARNISH

8 oz. frozen whipped topping,
  thawed

¼ cup walnuts, chopped

Pastry cutouts

Directions

For the crust: In a large bowl, combine flour, buttermilk powder, baking powder, and salt. With a pastry blender cut in Crisco until mixture resembles coarse crumbs. In a small bowl, beat egg, water, and vinegar together. With a pastry fork, add egg mixture slowly while tossing with fork until mixture is moistened (do not overmix). Divide dough and shape into 3 balls. Flatten each to form disc. Wrap each disc with plastic wrap and refrigerate at least 30 minutes before using. Makes 3 single crusts. Use one disc for this recipe. Roll out a single pastry and line a 9-inch pie dish. Crimp edge.

For the cream cheese layer: In a small mixing bowl, blend together cream cheese, sugar, and egg white until smooth. Sprinkle walnuts into bottom of unbaked pie shell and press into pastry gently. Spread cream cheese mixture over walnuts in bottom of pie shell.

For the filling: Preheat oven to 425°F. In a large mixing bowl, stir together sweet potato, eggs and yolk, brown sugar, maple syrup, milk, cinnamon, cloves, ginger, and salt until well blended. Pour mixture over cream cheese layer. Protect edge of pie with foil to prevent overbrowning. Bake at 425°F for 10 minutes. Reduce oven temperature to 350°F and bake 30 to 40 minutes or until center is set. Cool pie completely.

For the icing: In a small bowl, blend together cream cheese, powdered sugar, and milk until smooth. Drizzle or pipe over the top of cooled pie.

Pipe or dollop a ring of whipped topping around edge of pie; sprinkle with chopped walnuts and pastry cutouts, if desired. Chill until ready to serve.

Fall Splendor—Sweet Potato Pie in a Gingerbread Crust

Kathleen Harter, Hancock, MI 2011 APC Crisco National Pie Championships Amateur Division 1st Place Sweet Potato

Ingredients

CRUST

1½ cups unbleached King Arthur flour

½ cup brown sugar

1 teaspoon cinnamon

¼ teaspoon nutmeg

1 teaspoon ginger

1 teaspoon baking powder

½ teaspoon salt

2 teaspoons buttermilk powder

½ teaspoon lemon juice

½ cup toasted and finely chopped pecans

½ cup European-style butter, cold

1 tablespoon unsulfured organic molasses

3 tablespoons cold water

1 small egg white, lightly beaten (used on crust after baking)

FILLING

4 sweet potatoes

¼ cup European-style butter, melted

1 cup sugar

½ cup whole milk

2 eggs

½ teaspoon cinnamon

½ teaspoon nutmeg

½ teaspoon ginger

¼ teaspoon salt

1 teaspoon lemon extract

TOPPING

½ cup cream cheese, softened

¼ cup cooked sweet potato

1/8 teaspoon cinnamon

Dash nutmeg

Directions

For the crust: Mix all dry ingredients including the chopped pecans. Add molasses, lemon juice, and butter and mix just until the mixture resembles cornmeal. Add cold water and mix by hand until incorporated. Don't overmix.

Once blended, form into a ball, flatten slightly, wrap in plastic wrap and place in refrigerator for ½ hour to 1 hour. Remove from refrigerator and place on lightly floured surface. Roll dough into a circle that fits the pie plate. Place rolled crust into the pie plate, pressing into bottom edge and on fluted edges of pie plate. Use any remaining dough as a decorative element on top of assembled pie.

Use a fork to poke the bottom of pie plate before placing in freezer. Place crust in pie plate in freezer for a half hour. Preheat oven to 350°F. Remove pie plate from freezer and pre-bake in heated oven for 10 minutes. Once cooled, brush entire crust with lightly beaten egg white (helps to prevent fruit juices from soaking into crust).

For the filling: Preheat oven to 350°F. Peel and slice sweet potatoes into one-inch cubes.

Place in large saucepan, cover with water, and cook on medium heat until soft.

Drain water and place sweet potatoes in a large mixing bowl (reserving ¼ cup for topping). Using a paddle attachment of a stand mixer, add one egg at a time and then add spices, lemon extract, melted butter, and milk. Pour sweet potato filling into cooled crust. Bake pie for about 55 to 60 minutes, until a toothpick inserted in the middle comes out clean. Set aside and cool.

For the topping: Place all ingredients in a mixer and mix until well incorporated. Put topping in a piping bag and use a star point tip. Pipe topping in a pleasing design and decorate with additional pecans if desired.

Streusel-Topped Sweet Potato Pie

Sarah Spaugh, Winston-Salem, NC 2005 APC Crisco National Pie Championships Amateur Division 1ˢᵗ Place Sweet Potato

Ingredients

CRUST

2 cups all-purpose flour

¾ teaspoon salt

²/₃ cup butter-flavored Crisco shortening

5 to 6 tablespoons cold water

2 tablespoons melted butter

¾ cup whole milk

2 eggs

½ cup brown sugar

½ cup pure vanilla extract

¼ teaspoon salt

FILLING

3 to 4 sweet potatoes, cooked and peeled (2 cups mashed)

½ cup caramel sauce or ice cream topping

¾ teaspoon ground cinnamon

STREUSEL TOPPING

½ cup brown sugar

½ cup unsifted flour

¼ cup cold butter

¼ cup chopped pecans

Directions

For the crust: Combine flour and salt in a medium bowl. Cut in Crisco until flour is blended to form pea-sized crumbs. Sprinkle the cold water over the mixture and toss lightly with a fork until the dough forms a ball. Roll out the pastry and place it in a 9-inch pie plate.

For the filling: Preheat oven to 400°F. Spread the caramel sauce in the bottom of the unbaked pie crust. Mash the potatoes. Lightly beat the eggs. Add sugar to the eggs. Beat together and add to potatoes. Add and combine remaining ingredients. Pour into crust. Bake at 400°F for 15 minutes. Reduce heat to 350°F and bake for 30 more minutes. Remove the pie and sprinkle on the topping.

For the streusel topping: In a medium bowl, combine the brown sugar and flour. Cut in the butter until mixture is crumbly. Add the pecans. Sprinkle over pie. Bake for 10 to 15 minutes more or until the topping is golden brown. You may serve with whipped cream.

Sweet Potato Praline Cloud Pie

Beth Campbell, Belleville, WI 2003 APC Crisco National Pie Champion-ships Amateur Division 2003 1ˢᵗ Place Sweet Potato

Ingredients

CRUST

1 cup flour

½ cup shortening

Pinch of salt

¼ cup cold water

FILLING

2 sweet potatoes, baked or boiled

¼ cup butter, softened

1 cup sugar

2 eggs

½ teaspoon cinnamon

¼ teaspoon salt

½ teaspoon nutmeg

¼ teaspoon cloves

¼ teaspoon mace

1 cup evaporated milk

Meringue

¼ teaspoon salt

¼ teaspoon vanilla

1 teaspoon lemon juice

3 egg whites

6 tablespoons sugar

PRALINE TOPPING

2 tablespoons firmly packed dark
    brown sugar

2 tablespoons dark corn syrup

1 tablespoon butter

¼ teaspoon vanilla

⅓ cup chopped pecans

Directions

For the crust: Cut shortening into the flour and salt until it is pea-sized pieces, then add cold water, being careful not to over-blend. Chill for 30 minutes. Roll out and place into pie pan.

For the filling: Preheat oven to 350°F. Mash sweet potatoes and combine with all of the other ingredients. Pour into pie shell and bake until firm, about 35 to 40 minutes.

For the meringue: Separate eggs, and add 1ˢᵗ three ingredients to egg whites. Beat until foamy. Add 6 tablespoons sugar to the mixture, one tablespoon at a time. Beat until sugar dissolves.

For the topping: Preheat oven to 350°F. Combine brown sugar, syrup, butter, and vanilla in medium saucepan. Cook and stir on medium heat until butter is melted and mixture is blended. Remove from heat.

Spoon dollops of meringue in ring around outside edge of pie. Sprinkle ⅓ cup chopped pecans over the center of the pie. Drizzle all or part of the praline topping over the nuts, as desired. Bake for 15 minutes or until golden brown. Cool to room temperature before serving. Refrigerate leftover pie.

Sweet Potato Pie

Christine Montalvo, Windsor Heights, IA 2008 APC Crisco National Pie Championships Amateur Division 1st Place Sweet Potato

Ingredients

CRUST

2 cups all-purpose flour
1 cup cake flour
½ teaspoon salt
1/3 cup ice water
1 cup butter-flavored Crisco, frozen
  and cut into small pieces
1 large egg
1 teaspoon apple cider vinegar

FILLING

1 cup baked sweet potato (peeled),
  packed
3 eggs, slightly beaten
(2) 3 oz. packages cream cheese, softened
½ cup brown sugar
½ cup sugar
1 teaspoon vanilla
¼ cup butter, melted and cooled

Directions

For the crust: In food processor, combine the flours and salt. Add the shortening pieces and pulse until dough resembles coarse crumbs. Set aside. In a small bowl, beat together the egg, vinegar, and water. Add egg mixture to the flour mixture and combine with a fork, just until the dough comes together. Do not over mix. Form dough into 2 discs, wrap in plastic, and chill for at least one hour or overnight. Roll out one piece of pie crust into a 12-inch circle. Fit into a 9-inch deep-dish pie pan and flute edges. Set aside.

For the filling: Preheat oven to 350°F. Mash sweet potatoes. Add all the other ingredients to sweet potatoes and mix with mixer until smooth. Pour into pie shell. Bake for 20 to 30 minutes or until set. Remove from oven. Cool completely. Garnish with whipped cream.

INDEX

Conversion Charts

METRIC AND IMPERIAL CONVERSIONS

(These conversions are rounded for convenience)

Ingredient	Cups/Tablespoons/Teaspoons	Ounces	Grams/Milliliters
Butter	1 cup=16 tablespoons= 2 sticks	8 ounces	230 grams
Cream cheese	1 tablespoon	0.5 ounce	14.5 grams
Cornstarch	1 tablespoon	0.3 ounce	8 grams
Flour, all-purpose	1 cup/1 tablespoon	4.5 ounces/0.3 ounce	125 grams/8 grams
Flour, whole wheat	1 cup	4 ounces	120 grams
Fruit, dried	1 cup	4 ounces	120 grams
Fruits, chopped	1 cup	5 to 7 ounces	145 to 200 grams
Fruits, puréed	1 cup	8.5 ounces	245 grams
Honey, maple syrup, or corn syrup	1 tablespoon	.75 ounce	20 grams
Liquids: cream, milk, water, or juice	1 cup	8 fluid ounces	240 milliliters
Oats	1 cup	5.5 ounces	150 grams
Salt	1 teaspoon	0.2 ounce	6 grams
Spices: cinnamon, cloves, ginger, or nutmeg (ground)	1 teaspoon	0.2 ounce	5 milliliters
Sugar, brown, firmly packed	1 cup	7 ounces	200 grams
Sugar, white	1 cup/1 tablespoon	7 ounces/0.5 ounce	200 grams/12.5 grams
Vanilla extract	1 teaspoon	0.2 ounce	4 grams

OVEN TEMPERATURES

Fahrenheit	Celsius	Gas Mark
225°	110°	¼
250°	120°	½
275°	140°	1
300°	150°	2
325°	160°	3
350°	180°	4
375°	190°	5
400°	200°	6
425°	220°	7
450°	230°	8